JAGUAR IN COVENTRY
BUILDING THE LEGEND

Endpaper: *All Roads Lead to Jaguar.*
Covering the city's three main approaches
from London, Birmingham and Leicester
were 22 directional signs which brought
strangers to the city to the Jaguar works.
Nearly 18 months preliminary work,
including hundreds of interviews, had to be
carried out before the complete network
could be brought into operation. Some of
the original signs can still be seen today.

JAGUAR IN COVENTRY
BUILDING THE LEGEND

Nigel Thorley

Foreword by
Mike Beasley CBE

JAGUAR · DAIMLER
Heritage Trust

breedon **books**
P U B L I S H I N G

First published in Great Britain in 2002 by
The Breedon Books Publishing Company Limited
Breedon House, 3 The Parker Centre,
Derby, DE21 4SZ.

ISBN 1 85983 281 4

Printed and bound by Butler & Tanner, Frome,
Somerset, England.
Cover printing by Lawrence-Allen Colour Printers,
Weston-super-Mare, Somerset, England.

Contents

Acknowledgements

THE idea of writing this work on the history of the Jaguar company in Coventry came about because 2002 represents the 50th anniversary of the Browns Lane Jaguar plant in Allesley and both Breedon Books and the Jaguar Daimler Heritage Trust (JDHT) thought it an ideal opportunity to mark the occasion with a book on the subject. So I am most thankful to them for coming up with the initial idea.

As an author I am more accustomed to writing books and articles on aspects of the cars produced by the Jaguar company, than on the company itself. As such I found the task fascinating yet daunting as there was inevitably so much to cover and difficult decisions had to be taken on what to leave out rather than what to put in.

There are so many people and organisations I need to thank for their help in the preparation of this publication and I apologise now if I miss anyone out, it is certainly not intentional.

Firstly and most importantly, the Jaguar Daimler Heritage Trust and Jaguar Cars Limited for allowing me unlimited access to their extensive archive material and freedom to roam the factory to take photographs and talk to employees. Without their help and support this publication would not have been possible. I must also thank the many employees of Jaguar Cars both past and present for their enthusiasm and willingness to chat on all matters, and the other organisations within Jaguar, like the sports and social club and the long service association, who provided a lot of information.

Much credit must also be given to those who, in the past, kept excellent records, took photographs and produced publications like the *Jaguar Journal* and *Topics* (in-house magazines) from which some information was gleaned.

Again there are too many individuals to thank in a list but I would like to pay tribute to just a few who were particularly supportive. For example, two of the Jaguar Daimler Heritage Trust's volunteers who are also ex-Jaguar employees, Margaret and Derek Boyce. Their help in finding and identifying photographs was fantastic and they are a credit to Jaguar and the JDHT. Similarly, Julia Simpson spent time investigating the old roads of Coventry and then taking me on a tour of places of Jaguar interest. I thank Anders Clausager, the chief archivist at the JDHT, for his confidence and support, and I must mention a recent recruit to the JDHT, Karan Ram, who went to great trouble listing and scanning in images for me to use in this publication.

To everyone else thank you and I hope you enjoy this fascinating history of one of Coventry's greatest assets – Jaguar.

Nigel Thorley
Yorkshire, September 2002.

Foreword

by Mike Beasley, Executive Director Jaguar Cars Ltd

ON 28 November 1952, William Lyons invited his dealers and distributors, his key suppliers and the media to join him at Browns Lane, Allesley, Coventry. They were the first visitors to see the new home of Jaguar Cars.

Just days before he had put in place the final piece in a logistical jigsaw which saw the wholesale removal of all his company's manufacturing facilities and administrative staff two miles across Coventry. The relocation programme had taken well over a year and it had been achieved with the absolute minimum loss of production.

Jaguar, of course, had been in Coventry for 24 years before the move to Browns Lane. These were the formative years. Years of steady growth for the company which was still called SS Cars, and which had been founded by William Lyons with a £1,000 overdraft in Bloomfield Road, Blackpool in 1922.

In the spring of 1945, the company was finally and appropriately renamed Jaguar Cars. The universally acclaimed XK engine, which had been planned during the dark days of the Coventry blitz, meant that William Lyons no longer needed to rely on other manufacturers to power his cars. The XK120 had been introduced and was a runaway sales success and Jaguar's C-type sports cars had triumphed at Le Mans.

The move to Browns Lane signalled that Jaguar had changed gear. It was now an internationally recognised car manufacturer. The foundations had been laid for the company which today has major production facilities in Coventry, Birmingham and on Merseyside, a state-of-the-art engineering centre, and sells over 100,000 cars a year.

When I joined Jaguar over 25 years ago, Browns Lane had changed little since the early 1950s and today the view from my office is much the same as it was when occupied by Sir William. What has changed – and changed dramatically – are the manufacturing and assembly facilities. Like the company itself, they have been radically transformed. Progress has seen to that. Progress though, as Sir William Lyons said, literally days before he died in February 1985, never happens automatically – it must be earned.

How we have earned our progress is the story told by Nigel Thorley in this fascinating new book about Jaguar in Coventry. Nigel has drawn on his extensive knowledge of the company and its products and supplemented this with new material unearthed during extensive archival research.

It gives a new and welcome perspective to Jaguar's development in the city which has become our home, and very clearly demonstrates that our distinguished heritage has a vital role to play as we continue to grow for the future.

Mike Beasley

Introduction

by Anders Clausager, Chief Archivist Jaguar Daimler Heritage Trust

I AM very pleased to have been asked to contribute an introduction to Nigel Thorley's fascinating history of Jaguar in Coventry. This story would not be complete without reference also to how over many years we established the museum collection of vehicles, which is now the most prominent symbol of our company's pride in its heritage. This collection enables visitors to our Browns Lane plant to experience the history, heritage and passion which is Jaguar.

Among the more than 130 vehicles which we now preserve, the one that has been in our ownership for longest is the 1937 SS Jaguar saloon, which has never left us since it was originally used by Mrs Greta (Lady) Lyons. And as early as 1948, according to the records, we acquired an SS1 specifically for the 'museum'. This car is also still part of the collection.

This was soon followed by others, including an Austin Seven Swallow, Appleyard's XK120 rally car when it came back in 1953, and examples of the D-type. (It took another 30 years before we re-acquired a C-type!) These vehicles were usually displayed in the showroom in the new Browns Lane factory. In 1960, as part of the dowry of the Daimler company, we acquired an equally splendid collection of historic Daimler and Lanchester cars.

During the 1970s, the many collections of historic vehicles found within British Leyland were initially under threat, but Alex Park as the new chief executive in 1975 was more understanding and supported a joint display under the Leyland Historic Vehicles operation (later BL Heritage) in the museum at Donington Park. Even if this took some of Jaguar's heritage away from Browns Lane, at least the vehicles were now secure and were accessible to a wider public. The museum moved to Syon Park in London in 1981, and two years later a number of charitable educational trusts were set up to ensure preservation of the vehicles, artifacts and associated archives for the benefit of the nation. Thus in 1983 the present Jaguar Daimler Heritage Trust was established.

For some years, JDHT vehicles continued to be shown at Syon Park but the management of the trust and the collection were eventually brought back to Jaguar's home at Browns Lane. The collection grew steadily with further acquisitions of vehicles both old and new. Eventually it became clear that the JDHT needed a purpose-built home, which was opened by Sir Nicholas Scheele, our then chairman and managing director, in September 1998.

Today the JDHT has become established as the guardian of the heritage of Jaguar and Daimler. We are the corporate memory and conscience of Jaguar Cars Limited, a symbol of how important heritage is to the culture and philosophy of our company, today and for the future.

Anders Ditlev Clausager

The Jaguar Daimler
Heritage Trust
Heritage Centre on
the Browns Lane
site. They are the
custodians of the
Jaguar and allied
companies' archives
and vehicles.

Chapter One

Background to a Legend

I T IS sad to reflect that so few of the famous names in British car manufacture have survived and this has naturally had an adverse affect on the Coventry area, generally considered to be the home of the motor industry in the UK. Names like Alvis, Armstrong-Siddeley, Hillman, Humber, Lea Francis, Standard, Triumph and many more were synonymous with Coventry yet they are no more. It is fortunate and

Sir William Lyons, the co-founder of the business and genius behind Jaguar, is seen here with his wife Greta and dog Sally at their Wappenbury Hall home in Warwickshire. Sir William passed away in 1985.

somewhat ironic therefore that one company which did not have its origins in Coventry has stood the test of time and has not only survived but prospered, bringing wealth and success to the area – Jaguar.

While the Coventry origins of one of Jaguar's companies, the Daimler Company Ltd, go back to before the turn of the last century, Jaguar, or should we say its forerunner Swallow, originated in another part of the country, Blackpool in Lancashire. Then called the Swallow Sidecar Company, it was established in 1922 by the partnership of William Lyons and William Walmsley. Lyons was the son of a family with a musical business in the town and Walmsley was the son of a retired coal merchant from Stockport who had moved to and lived in the same street in Blackpool as Lyons.

Walmsley was the craftsman of the two and already had experience refurbishing motorcycles. He was trying to run a one-man business from the garage of his home making and selling sidecars. Lyons (the younger of the two partners) was the entrepreneur. It was at his suggestion that the partnership was formed as he appreciated the business opportunity building and selling stylish sidecars to keen motorcyclists presented. Cars were still very expensive and out of the reach of most people at that time.

Initially operating from the upstairs floor of a small site to the south of the town, the business prospered, despite a shortage of cash, and after taking on supplementary rented accommodation around the area, they eventually, in 1926, took on extensive premises in Cocker Street. At that time William Lyons decided that they ought to be building bodies on cars as well as sidecars.

By purchasing an Austin 7 chassis from a dealer in Lancashire Swallow were able to hand-craft a rather attractive curvaceous body onto the little Austin which, with the aid of bright two-tone paintwork, would prove to be very appealing. Eventually the Henlys organisation (one of the country's leading motor car distributors) took up the option to finance the purchase of rolling chassis from the Austin Motor Company which Swallow would then body, whereupon Henlys would distribute and sell them.

This coincided with a change in the name of the company to the Swallow Sidecar and Coachbuilding Company, emphasising the new aspect of the business. The success of the little Austin Swallow was virtually instant and at one stage the railway marshalling yard in Blackpool was embarrassingly full of chassis awaiting body fitment. This success led to the introduction of a second model, the Austin Swallow saloon, and other cars also began to be bodied, some from Coventry makers like Standard. Then, in 1928, the decision was taken to move the whole business away from Blackpool. The lack of skilled labour and the transportation costs of materials were problems in Blackpool, and a move to the West Midlands would be very beneficial in terms of access to a good supply of labour, raw materials and specialist services for the motor industry, which was centred in that part of the country.

A site was chosen at Foleshill and the move was completed in 1928. Several of the original workforce from Blackpool elected to relocate to Coventry to stay with the company. With a larger site, better facilities and continued growth, the company decided to expand into proper car production and in 1931 the first of their new products was announced. A deal was struck with the well-respected Coventry motor manufacturer Standard to supply completed chassis to Swallow. These would be bodied and trimmed to a new sporty style and marketed under the name SS. The SS1 and a second, smaller vehicle, the SS2, were distributed alongside the Swallow-bodied cars through the Henlys organisation. Sidecar production also continued in Coventry at this time.

Over the next few years the business continued to expand, as did the SS model range, although all production was based on the same mechanical theme. Then in 1934 the partnership between Lyons and Walmsley broke up, and Lyons bought Walmsley's share of the business. At the same time a new company was set up, SS Cars Limited, alongside the existing business, emphasising the concentration on car production while Swallow continued to produce sidecars.

It was not until September 1935 that the name Jaguar first appeared, applied to a new SS saloon car model launched at that time, supplemented by the first true sports car in the range, the SS Jaguar 100. From this point, until the outbreak of World War Two, the company continued to expand and indeed over 20,000 cars were produced up to 1940 using the Jaguar model name. From then on SS Cars and Swallow were, like most other companies, totally immersed in the war effort, although William Lyons and his small engineering team were quietly working on proposals for post-war car production alongside their war responsibilities.

After the war the sidecar part of the business was sold off and SS Cars Limited became Jaguar Cars Ltd, which led to the dropping of the SS insignia from the vehicles. This was the first time that the name Jaguar was used in its own right as the brand marque instead of just a model name. However, it was not until 1948 that the company was able to produce its first entirely new post-war car, the XK120 sports, followed in 1950 by a mass-production prestige saloon, the Mark VII, both using Jaguar's first unique, 6-cylinder engine.

By 1951 William Lyons had negotiated to take over a Daimler 'shadow' factory in Allesley into which all production would be transferred, abandoning the by then vastly expanded Foleshill works. Jaguar's on-going success in the 1950s is legendary and will be covered in more detail later in this book; suffice it to say at this point that the Browns Lane site quickly developed and expanded to meet the needs of what was becoming one of the country's most prestigious motor manufacturers, culminating in 1956 with William Lyons receiving a knighthood for his work in the industry.

In 1960 Jaguar purchased the Daimler Company Ltd, the oldest surviving motor manufacturer in the country and a company with a tremendous heritage both in the provision of private cars to royalty and the gentry, and in the supply of commercial and military vehicles through two world wars. Daimler and its Radford factory continued to play a major role in the Jaguar Group alongside other companies like Guy Motors, Coventry Climax and Henry Meadows. In 1968 Jaguar joined forces with the British Motor Corporation (BMC) to form British Motor Holdings, and later another major move brought virtually the whole of the British motor industry under the one banner of British Leyland.

Generally considered to be very bad times for Jaguar and the British motor industry, many companies did not survive the upheaval and a lot has to be said for the integrity of the long-term Jaguar workforce in helping the company through this traumatic period, aided by a new man at the helm, John Egan. Jaguar was eventually separated from British Leyland and privatised in 1984. Sir William Lyons died in 1985, although he was able to see the company return to self-control. A new site was acquired in Whitley that became Jaguar's engineering facility, which continues to expand to this day. Jaguar also took control of its body making facility at Castle Bromwich in Birmingham, formerly part of the Pressed Steel Company, and a brand new model in 1986 (the XJ40) led the company to further success.

The Ford Motor Company purchased Jaguar Cars Limited in 1990, since which time significant investment has been put into the business. This has led to a redevelopment of the Castle Bromwich site, further expansion at Whitley, the refurbishment of the Browns Lane assembly line and new office accommodation. The company has also further expanded its operations with the takeover of the old Ford factory in Halewood, Liverpool, for the production of the smaller X-type range, although Jaguar and Ford are still committed to the West Midlands and Coventry in particular, which is the real home of Jaguar and the location of its head office and assembly area for the flagship XJ saloons and XK sports cars.

Chapter Two

The Formative Pre-Coventry Years – 1922 to 1928

I T IS not the intention of this publication to cover the whole of Jaguar's history but more to concentrate on the important period from 1928 to the present day and the company's involvement in and around Coventry. However it is necessary to review the early years of the business, its development and the reasoning behind the move to the West Midlands.

The key figure in our story is William Lyons, co-founder of the company and Blackpool bred. He initially took up an apprenticeship at Crossley Motors in Manchester, although he didn't stay the term and ended up returning to Blackpool to sell motorcycles. From the family home in King Edward Avenue, Blackpool, Lyons (then only 20 years of age) befriended neighbour William Walmsley, 10 years his senior.

William Walmsley was already in business of sorts making stylish sidecars under the name Swallow from his parents' garage at the rear of the house. This was 1921 and with little business acumen Walmsley did not have the temperament or guidance to move the one-man business forward. William Lyons, on the other hand, saw an excellent opportunity to develop this into a commercial business and between the two families it was agreed to set up as the Swallow Sidecar Company with capital acquired from both fathers.

Business commenced on the upper floors of small industrial premises in Bloomfield Road with later additions in the surrounding area to cope with the need for storage space.

Swallow bought in chassis from other manufacturers and here the first connections with Coventry came about.

Where it all started in Bloomfield Road, Blackpool: the first building utilised by the Swallow Sidecar Company in 1922.

Swallow moved to this site in Cocker Street, Blackpool, in 1926, changing the name of the company to the Swallow Sidecar and Coachbuilding Company. An example of their production sidecar can be seen to the right of the building.

Montgomery's, a chassis makers local to Coventry, were appointed to supply chassis to the small Blackpool concern.

The business grew to the point that it had outlived its myriad small premises and the need for both money and space led to William Walmsley's father leasing them a building he had acquired in Cocker Street, Blackpool, providing adequate room for expansion. This brought about the change in name from the Swallow Sidecar Company to the Swallow Sidecar and Coachbuilding Company, and, along with it, an aggressive plan to acquire more skilled labour as sidecar production grew to around 100 per week. Labour was difficult to find in Blackpool so Swallow advertised further afield, even as far as Coventry, in the hope of encouraging skilled workers to move to the seaside, although this strategy met with limited success.

One Midlands man joining Swallow was Cyril Holland, who drew up a rough design for a stylish coachbuilt body which Lyons was immediately attracted to. He decided to build a prototype of the design on an Austin 7 chassis he had acquired from an Austin

Contemporary drawing of the original Swallow body design for the Austin Seven shown with a fitted hard top that cost the owner an extra £10 at the time.

(and Swallow sidecar) dealer in Lancashire. The end result was the beautifully stylish Austin Swallow, announced in the spring of 1927 as a two-seater sporting version of the Austin 7 with or without a fitted hard top. Selling initially through some of the sidecar agents, by mid-1927 a Morris Cowley version of the Swallow body was also offered and William Lyons set his sights further afield. A visit to Birmingham resulted in a 50-car order with P.J. Evans Limited, and after consultation with the

The later and more successful saloon version of the Austin Seven Swallow. Two-tone paint finishes, unusual on this class of car at the time, were initially available in a very limited range of colours and were expanded in the early 1930s.

Henlys organisation in London a mammoth order for 500 Austin Swallows was received, which would break the back of the little Cocker Street factory in Blackpool.

By this time the number of employees in Blackpool had reached 50, including those who had moved up from the Midlands, but this was nowhere near enough to cope with the extra demand, particularly as part of the Henlys deal was to provide another version, a saloon model of the Austin Swallow. William Lyons considered a further move locally but then, realising the need for skilled labour, made frequent trips to the West Midlands and finally decided on a suitable site. When he announced the move to the Blackpool workforce over 30 of the 50 employees agreed to relocate with him and the company to Coventry. The complete factory move from Blackpool to Coventry was planned for 1928.

Chapter Three

Inland to the Midlands and SS to Jaguar – 1928 to 1939

THE move from Blackpool to Coventry took some considerable time to organise, not least because Swallow could not at the time afford to purchase premises, instead having to find somewhere on a rental or lease basis that was sufficiently large for their current operation and capable of expansion as the business grew.

Lyons's decision to move to Coventry was purely down to logistics, even though the city was over 140 miles away from the then 'home' of Swallow. With most major motor manufactures like Standard based in Coventry, along with significant parts suppliers, engineering businesses and such all within a few miles radius, it was the hub of the motor industry.

Lyons, and sometimes Walmsley, made frequent visits to Coventry during 1927 and 1928 looking for potential factory sites. On these trips they stayed at the Queen's Hotel in Hertford Street, an establishment that no longer exists.

Although the two men considered alternatives like Wolverhampton, Coventry was ideal for the reasons mentioned above. Lyons found a site that appealed to him in the north of the city around the Foleshill, Holbrook and Radford areas (close to the existing giant Daimler factory and other good local industry). A large area known as the Whitmore Park Estate was owned and run by a cartel, which Lyons came to know about through their secretary, Harry Gillitt.

Part of the complex of buildings were four shed-like blocks built during the 1914–18 war, two of which had been used for the manufacture of shells and other armaments. Left abandoned since the war, they were in usable condition but required significant renovation. The two other blocks were then occupied by a company called Holbrook Bodies (who at the time worked for another Coventry car manufacturer, Hillman). On the same site were other useful contacts for Swallow: the Dunlop Rim and Wheel Company, Motor Panels Limited and an engineering business, White and Poppe Ltd.

An agreement was struck for Swallow to lease just one of the blocks for the modest sum, even in those days, of £1,200 per year over a three-year period, then to have the option to purchase both it and another building later. The site was off Holbrook Lane, with a Foleshill postal address, accessed via an unmade lane that would later be called Swallow Road for obvious reasons. The move to Foleshill took place in the autumn and winter of 1928, not the best time to take possession of a new factory without proper heating or lighting, with an unmade road for access. There was also the problem of co-ordinating transportation over a distance of 140 miles.

Generally in a pretty poor state of repair, the building required a lot of renovation work and although a quote was obtained for a local contractor to carry out the work, Lyons, on behalf of Swallow, declined. He instead followed his by then established procedure of organising the labour to carry out repairs and maintenance himself, a situation that continued for many years. Lyons advertised locally for people to do the work and was inundated with replies as unemployment was so bad in Coventry at that time.

The work involved major repairs, not least to the roof, although many members of staff continually complained about leaks when it rained years later. In fact the factory, although quite adaptable for motor car production, was never actually ideal. There were no provisions made to extract exhaust fumes or prevent build up of damp, even in the later years of occupation.

Those workers who opted to move to Coventry from Blackpool, including some who had their origins in the area, were not provided with any incentive to make the transition, save for an increase in working hours that was required to get production underway in the new building. Despite a higher cost of living in the West Midlands there was no extra pay or incentive to make the move in the form of relocation allowance – something that would be unthinkable today!

Swallow had never experienced a high turnover of workers in Blackpool, perhaps because of the lack of jobs available in the town. Given the significant number of workers who made the momentous move to Coventry, it was clear that even in these early days, Lyons, Walmsley and the company benefited from a great deal of loyalty from their staff. However, there was an urgent need for more labour, and so advertisements were placed locally. This resulted in a mob of applicants, many of whom had previously worked in the industry but had fallen on hard times. Although it was impossible to employ everyone, this constant stream of ready labour ensured that

Aerial photograph of the Holbrook Lane industrial site, c.1928. The four sets of rectangular shed buildings in the top left-hand corner of the picture are the units taken up by Swallow and later SS. The two small buildings facing the opposite direction to and in front of the main sheds were the offices. The road following the buildings from the top left of picture across the centre and joining Holbrook Lane to the right hand side of the picture is Swallow Road, adopted and made good by SS for access to their part of the complex.

Swallow managed to get together a good, well-trained, skilled workforce with little difficulty.

The workforce was not without its problems, however, as industrial relations did not get off to a good start. Lyons, a stickler for hard work, was frugal and totally committed to getting the job done. These aims had resulted, just before the move, in the introduction of a piece-work scheme affecting most employees. The principles were that William Lyons crudely evaluated the time it took to do each task and then, working back from the average weekly pay, divided that by the number of those tasks that could be performed in the working week, arriving at a figure. For each task a worker was given a book of paper vouchers. Upon completion of a task the worker signed one voucher, which was duly counter-signed by his foreman and then torn off, signifying the completion of that job.

At the end of each day the vouchers were returned to the wages office and from these the weekly pay was made up.

It was a simplistic but basically sound system, which meant that Swallow had total control over the costing of each job. It also supposedly gave the workers the opportunity to earn more based on how hard they worked. The Blackpool people were used to the system. Although the 'new' Coventry workers were informed of this principle and abided by it, after the first week there was general disgust at the poor state of their wage packets because they had not been working to the speed intended, so fewer tasks had been completed, resulting in lower pay. Disgruntled employees took over the spares office where the vouchers were kept and dumped them out over the floor. This must have been the first 'dispute' for Swallow and Lyons.

William Lyons spoke to everyone about how the system worked and explained that if the workers did their jobs properly, they could earn substantially more than on a day rate. He also pointed out that he was not going to change the system. However, a compromise was reached. Lyons paid a day-rate for just one week, by the end of which most of the workers had grasped the idea of the new system and realised that they could still earn reasonable money. It should, however, be said that for most of the time at Foleshill employees worked longer hours than workers with other companies, presumably not only to meet the demand for cars but also to ensure a good week's pay! After the dispute notices started to appear around the factory saying 'No Day Work Paid'.

Another early dispute involved union membership in the sawmill, which resulted in the first withdrawal of labour. Although it was then still difficult to find the right type of skilled worker to fulfill the sawmill tasks, Lyons advertised elsewhere in the country to find replacements for those who caused trouble, who were promptly given their cards.

During these initial months the two partners, Lyons and Walmsley, stayed in lodgings in St Paul's Road, near Foleshill. Their families remained in Blackpool until things were more settled. The business was soon up and running, initially assembling cars from parts coming down from Blackpool and then, as the workforce grew, completed cars were built entirely in Foleshill. Numbers of Swallows turned out by the end of the first

year rose significantly from 12 to 40 a week and along with this the model range also expanded.

The new models were the Alvis Swallow, the Fiat Swallow and the Swift Swallow. The latter model would be the most prestigious (and the most expensive at £269) car the company would produce under the Swallow banner. However, it was to be short-lived, as the Swift company went into receivership in 1931. There was some concern over the continued availability of Austin Seven chassis on which to build Swallow bodies, which was one reason why Lyons moved into other makes, although never in anything like the numbers of Austins.

As time passed by, sales continued to improve and as the 1930s began Swallow became generally a more professional business. Another model appeared with a Swallow body, a car that would hold some significance for the company in this decade, the Standard Swallow. This was followed by the Wolseley Hornet Swallow, a much more sporty car with a six-cylinder engine.

The country was still very much in depression at this stage, even though Swallow themselves were doing well, not just on the car body side, but also with sidecars, many of which benefited from the use of wood left-overs from the building of car bodies, therefore keeping costs down considerably for the company as a whole. Building processes had changed at Swallow after the move from Blackpool. For example, the old wooden body frame building methods of cutting each piece from a solid,

Sidecar production at Foleshill was separated from car work. On the stillages can be seen formers for the different styles of sidecar produced at the time.

Joinery was an important part of early car body production, continued from the carriage days. Here a complete side of an SS1 body is being assembled on a former. Skilled joiners were always in strong demand before the introduction of the all-steel body construction methods.

individually shaping it to fit a specific body, took too much time. A modern system already used in the area was the steam-bent process, which allowed wood to be cut and shaped in large quantities and bodies built on prepared jigs. Although there were major problems implementing the process, which at one point stopped production, eventually it worked and dramatically improved efficiency. Generally a more modernistic approach was made to assembly that even involved a change in painting process from hand application and varnish to cellulose spray.

By early 1930 the two partners had moved to more permanent accommodation. William Walmsley moved to Belvedere Road, not far from the factory, to a house he called Swallowdene, and Lyons bought 5, Eastleigh Avenue, Earlsdon, also not far

away, although he only stayed a year, moving to a house called Woodside on Gibbet Hill in a more palatial part of the city. It was at this time that Swallow Coachbuilding became a limited company. With the future looking good Lyons took the decision to buy the second of the sheds on the Foleshill site.

Arranging a mortgage with the local Coventry Permanent Building Society, both this and the first building were purchased, providing a total of some 80,000 square feet.

By 1931 Lyons had been in negotiation with the relatively new boss at one of Coventry's largest companies and a well-respected car producer, Standard at Canley. Captain John Black was approached with a view to an expansion of the Swallow business, from bodying existing chassis for individual customers, to buying an exclusively adapted chassis from Standard to be bodied by Swallow, forming the basis of a Swallow car, to be called the SS. A new insignia, incorporating the initials, would be adopted by the company for its own line in motor cars.

The idea was for William Lyons to move the company into car production under its own brand name. It was a natural progression of the business and one that would have proved necessary anyway if the company were to prosper. However, it was still a risky affair, as at the same time other local companies like Riley and Triumph were already in trouble and even Bentley at Cricklewood eventually went to the wall, only to be

Part of the paint shop at Foleshill. Paint mixing facilities can be seen at the back of the room and the bodies were manoeuvered on wheeled dollies. Note the lack of air extraction equipment or face protection in those days.

The main body assembly shop at Foleshill with various
models of Swallow under construction. The 'shed' style of
building was never totally ideal because of the roof support
pillars that infringed on working areas. No moving tracks
are in place at this point, just wooden slats in the floor to
guide the wheels along in a straight line.

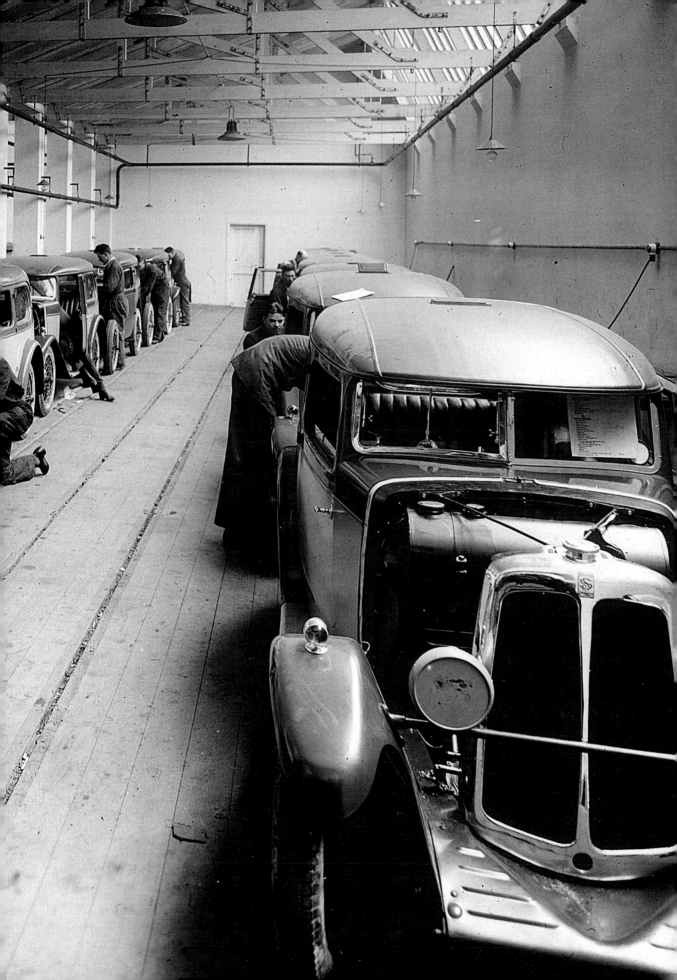

drawn in to Rolls-Royce. Sales of the little Austin Swallows were already starting to decline as the model was over five years old, and, with the demise of Swift and Fiat business, this left only Wolseley, where cars were produced in very small numbers and, of course, Standards with Swallow bodies. So there was an urgent need to build up business relations with a large formidable company like Standard and to involve them in the provision of chassis for the company.

At this point it is worth considering what the insignia SS actually meant as there has been much discussion about this over the years. Its origins must, to some extent, lie in Lyons's fondness for the Brough Superior motorcycle and the SS80 model that he once owned. To some, however, (particularly the Standard Motor Company) SS stood for Standard Swallow, a natural assumption.

For others it meant Swallow Sports or Swallow Special, so a lot depends on whose side you are on. There has never been a definitive answer, other than an interview the author once read, given by William Lyons many years ago, which indicated Swallow Sports to be near enough right.

Returning to the issue of car production, the chassis chosen was the Standard Sixteen, modified to suit Swallow's requirements and fitted with a choice of 2-litre or 2.5-litre six-cylinder engines. Swallow had to pay an initial £500 to Standard for tooling and agreed to take 500 chassis in the first year at a price of £130 for the SS1 (as it would become known) and £82 for the SS2 (a much smaller chassis and running gear based around the Standard Nine). This represented a lot of cars and, of course, money, but Lyons was, as ever, confident that he could make a success of the deal. Local firm Motor Panels, based on the same estate as Swallow, was given the work of supplying body panels for the new cars and deals were struck around the area for other components and bought-in assemblies.

The new SS models hit the Olympia motor show in 1931 to national acclaim. The SS1 was a long, low car although its final design did not totally meet with Lyons's approval. Due to the removal of his appendix during the final prototype build stage his partner, Walmsley, had decided to raise the roof height to enable easier entry and exit for driver and passenger and this changed the ultra-low slung attitude of Lyons's original design.

The first car produced under the SS name, the SS1 from 1932 had cycle wings and an elongated bonnet, giving the impression of more power than the little car really had.

Of six-cylinder engine capacity, the SS1 was initially rated at 16hp, powered through a four-speed gearbox, while the smaller SS2, being a scaled-down model stylistically, used the four-cylinder 9hp engine and a three-speed crash gearbox.

Sales of the new SS cars were buoyant, and the 500 chassis that were part of the initial deal with Standard were built and sold from 1932 to 1933 despite numerous problems with quality control and longevity of parts. In those

days Swallow had no engineering design department or means of thoroughly testing products.

With the growth of car production, Swallow moved into 1933 with their sights set on further expansion. The opportunity came to buy the other two sheds on the site, used by Holbrook Bodies, who, by this time, had gone out of business. Early in 1933 Lyons purchased the pair of buildings for £12,000. The company had made a handsome profit of that sum the previous year and, with expectations of even better profits (£22,000 in 1933), Lyons felt justified. His and Swallow's commitment to Coventry was complete. He had purchased all four buildings on the estate and had moved his bank account from Blackpool to Lloyds in Coventry.

Sidecar production was still very important to the company at this time and sales in this area were also encouraging. Lyons had employed a Wolverhampton motorcycle specialist, Howard Raymond Davies, as marketing manager, and although the Sidecar name was quietly dropped from the title Swallow, sidecars still accounted for a large proportion of company profits. Chassis were still bought in, but by 1933 the Coventry company Grindlays was the chosen supplier.

The SS1 and SS2 motor cars were already undergoing further development, which was to culminate in the 1933 motor show appearance of the two substantially

The smaller SS2 produced around the Standard Nine chassis. A rear-mounted spare wheel, fabric covered roof and two-tone paintwork gave the car an air of luxury for a modest £210.

upgraded cars. Longer in the chassis, with new swept back wings and more powerful engines, the cars now depicted the brand new monogrammed SS logo design which would become the norm in all publicity for the cars in future. By the time the revised SS models came onto the market Swallow had over 100 dealers in the UK and many abroad, with export sales also proving healthy.

Later in the same year the last Wolseley Hornet Swallows were produced, bringing to an end Swallow body production as a separate entity. All production would now be turned over to SS1 and SS2 models (plus sidecars of course) and at this time the first of several additional SS1 models became available. The Tourer was effectively the SS1 with the roof cut off, a sporty wooden-framed hood and cut-away doors. It was not long before a third SS1 variant came to the market, the saloon, offering extra windows in the rear compartment at a slightly premium price. The SS2s subsequently received the same treatment as the SS1s, with a longer chassis, a larger engine with a full four-speed gearbox and swept-back wings. Also made available in saloon and tourer form, they sold in relatively small numbers compared to the larger cars.

It was at this stage that another Coventry company became involved with Swallow. The Coventry Motor Cylinder Company provided specially made aluminium cylinder heads for the Standard engines fitted to the SS models. Through them William Lyons met a man called Harry Weslake, an independent engineer who would subsequently redesign all the cylinder heads used on the Standard engines for SS cars, dramatically improving performance. This meant a conversion to overhead valves, leading Lyons to form, for the first time, his own engineering department at the Swallow factory.

Relations between Lyons and Walmsley had, by this time, become strained, and they both agreed that Walmsley should retire from the business. Thus, in October 1933 a new company was formed, called SS Cars Limited, which was incorporated into a public company with a capital of £250,000. The combined profits for the business over the three years leading up to July 1934 amounted to £72,500 with net assets shown as £179,857. William Lyons was now in total control of the business which would shortly move forward to another level of success in Coventry.

At around the same time a new man joined the Swallow team. Ernest Rankin had tremendous experience in promoting General Motors and Watneys products. Commonly known as 'Bill' Rankin (because of his middle name) he substantially improved the marketing of the SS name with the launch of an *SS Magazine*, a close relationship with the then new SS Car Club and the development of PR affairs locally, nationally and internationally. By now SS cars were also performing well on the competition scene, providing another string to Rankin's bow in marketing the cars and company.

A service department was also formed, albeit in a space between buildings covered as a lean-to. A small team of men worked hard to develop this important side of the business, bringing the customers closer to the company.

More skilled labour joined the SS team as another company on the estate, White and Poppe Engineers moved. Their operation moved southwards, and important and talented engineers from that factory joined SS Cars, providing valuable input on engineering techniques. A tool room was set up to provide various small body components to avoid the extra cost of buying such items in and so the business moved forward with ever-increasing zeal and decreasing dependency on other companies.

The 1934 motor show saw the company run its own stand, to display its widening range of SS1 and SS2 models. This included a new Airline model, based on a streamlined design, taking features from the Art Deco era. The car gained significant attention and was to be the centrepiece of the range for a couple of years.

Lyons was a hard task-master and the workers were still toiling six days a week and longer than normal hours. Average pay was about £5 per week for a skilled man, and SS were paying less than other local businesses. However, if they worked hard, using their piece-work system, men could earn substantially more. Not only the manual workers had to put in the hours. The office staff was small and had to cope with everything from taking orders to enquiries, dealing with suppliers, letters and so on, and since the phones were always busy, they sometimes had to manage their routine work after 5pm at night.

Lyons did have a streak of kindness though. For example, he organised an annual trip to Blackpool for the employees. This was paid for by the company and he, along with other managers, accompanied the parties. This must have been quite an

One of the annual outings to Blackpool for SS employees sponsored by the company. These events were well supported, and after the frolics of the seaside, a sit-down dinner was enjoyed in the Tower.

experience for most employees, as in those days holidays were far from the norm, perhaps the maximum of one week a year, and if one took a holiday, it was at one's own expense and with loss of pay.

In the 1934 financial year the company built a total of 1,724 cars and for the following year another new SS1 model joined the range, the drophead coupé, a design much admired and akin to a contemporary Rolls-Royce Continental (but at a significantly lower price). This was short-lived and only about 100 were produced.

By this time the engineering department was coming into its own and Harry Weslake had been working on revised Standard engines for the later cars. Another local man came to Jaguar, this time from Humber, in the form of William Heynes, another engineer by profession. The team was readying itself for another major move forward, and Heynes was made the first chief engineer of SS Cars Ltd.

However, problems still abounded in some areas, particularly with bought-in supplies. For example, on one occasion Standard let the company down over the supply of chassis, which slowed down or even halted some areas of SS assembly for a number of weeks. It was very difficult in those days to smoothly bring together all aspects of manufacture, not least for a very small company like SS, among the might of 'more important' customers in Coventry.

The prominent SS insignia on the office wall and the very substantial oak doors, also depicting the logo. An appropriate SS Jaguar saloon stands outside.

During this time Foleshill was constantly upgraded and improved. By now SS had been forced to shell out for a proper road surface on the access road, as with constant use it had become more and more difficult to get people, let alone vehicles with supplies, down to the factory. That monogrammed SS image now appeared in full glory above the doors of the main office block, itself rebuilt, and SS occupied all four of the original buildings offered to them back in 1928.

At an extraordinary general meeting of the company on 30 November 1935 the capital of the company was increased to £350,000. Another new company was registered that year, the Swallow Coachbuilding Company (1935) Ltd, to deal separately with the sidecar business. Inaugurated with £10,000 worth of capital, this company would see sidecar production through to the post-war period.

It was important to keep the ball rolling with car manufacture, and in order not to rest on his laurels William Lyons decreed that a new car should be produced with a unique name to further the company's position as a manufacturer of luxury, prestige, fast yet economical motor cars. While Weslake, Heynes and the rest of the team were working on a new coachbuilt saloon, Lyons set about deciding on a name for the car and with the help of an advertising agency came up with the name Jaguar to epitomise the type of car he wanted to build.

Although SS had very few engineering facilities at this time, Lyons nonetheless decided to produce the design of the new chassis in-house, from which completed units would be made up for the company by Rubery Owen and assembled as rolling units with engines by Standard. To do this SS made up a mock chassis in wood from which Standard made the drawings to work from. The principle of the new chassis was to be low-slung in nature, enabling SS to design a sporting body to fit. Onto the chassis Standard would fit their 16hp engine, a gearbox and a rear axle, in the form of a 'rolling chassis'. Permission to use the name Jaguar was gained from another Coventry company, Armstrong-Siddeley, who held the rights to the name for an aero engine, and deadlines were set for the launch of the new model.

An example of how William Lyons designed his cars. Joiners and metal workers would fabricate individual panels and fit them temporarily with the aid of wooden planks and supports in order for Lyons to evaluate the effect, a procedure that continued through to the 1960s. This is a mock-up of what would become the first Jaguar, the SS Jaguar 2.5-litre saloon.

Initial testing of the new engine was carried out by using an existing SS1 tourer model, and Standard agreed to pay for the tooling and to manufacture the new 2.7-litre six-cylinder engine to Weslake's design specifically for SS Cars. They would continue to supply their four-cylinder side-valve engine for a smaller version of the new saloon. Body jigs were set up for the new design although most of the individual body panels were still bought in from Motor Panels, also on the Foleshill site. By this time Triumph cars had moved into part of the plant once occupied by the engineering company, so there was increased competition for the services of surrounding businesses.

The SS Jaguar six-cylinder saloon was finally launched in September 1935, along with a four-cylinder version. The name Jaguar had appeared for the first time, although at this stage it was still a model name as opposed to a marque brand.

A few SS1s and SS2s continued to be produced over the first months of SS Jaguar production, although by 1936 all assembly at Foleshill revolved around the new saloons, the renamed SS Jaguar tourer and a new low-production sports car called the SS Jaguar 100. Based essentially on a shortened version of the saloon with the Weslake engine, the '100' offered a degree of panache for the company and became well respected on the competition front, although it only remained in production until the outbreak of World War Two.

To meet the anticipated and received demand for the SS Jaguar, a new moving assembly line was devised and installed at Foleshill which was chain driven. This enabled the bodies to be mounted on constantly moving jigs while the operatives assembled the various components. There was some resentment about this as it meant workers had to maintain pace alongside the cars.

The early success of the SS Jaguar resulted in a rise in profits to over £34,000 in 1937 and total production of 3,637 cars, providing the best ever dividend for share holders at the time of 12.5 percent. This success also enabled the Lyons family to move out of Coventry to Leamington Spa and their final home, Wappenbury Hall.

SS Cars was still expanding and taking on more and more staff, many of whom came directly from other car manufacturing businesses in Coventry and the surrounding areas. Some came from Standard, which must have caused some embarrassment at the time because of the strong link between the two companies. With the anticipated increase in work, the staffing level rose to over 1,500, coinciding with a major change in production practice.

The SS Jaguar saloons were initially built in the time-honoured way of grafting steel and alloy panels onto an ash frame produced on a jig. This was time consuming and led to much hand fitting to get everything just right. The rate of sale for the new car was so great that the company could not meet its orders without a move, following other manufacturers, to all-steel body production.

Even at this stage SS did not have the finances or sales figures to embark on the production of an all-steel body from one of the specialist makers, so many small panels were to be made up by outside businesses. A trial body was made up in steel and then dissected into its various panels, which were all produced by different companies, causing a problem. For example, the doors and roof came from Rubery Owen, Sankey produced the quarter panels and a number of other companies were also involved with various aspects of the new body. In the meantime the production line was modified to take advantage of the new body building techniques in preparation and all the staff were prepared for the change.

During this time the new all-steel models were announced to the public at the

motor show in 1937. The new style body necessitated slight changes in dimensions and trim, the movement of the side-mounted spare wheel to the boot, the change of the four-cylinder engine to overhead valves and the arrival of another new model, the 3.5-litre saloon, with an even larger version of the Weslake engine.

The factory, however, although ready for production, had to virtually shut down due to problems over the fit of the different panels to make up the body whole. It took months to put matters right, which with all the companies involved inevitably cost SS dearly in sales and lost revenue, resulting in a fall in profits for the year. Out of the ashes came their most successful model yet and the birth of a new type of craftsman to replace the age-old coachbuilders art. Panel fit was still by no means perfect, and a lot of hand finishing work was involved in the production of the new car, although this did not tend to slow production down too much. Lead loading became the norm, a practice carried on well into the 1980s by Jaguar and other manufacturers. Along with the 'productionised' saloons, however, there was a limited production run of drophead coupés based on the same body design but with only two doors and a hood mechanism which would continue to be produced by the old coachbuilding methods even after World War Two. By 1938 production was meeting sales to the point where

The engine test facility at Foleshill with examples of both four and six-cylinder engines on test.

The pre-war trim shop at Foleshill, still predominantly manned by male workers. In later years women would dominate this department.

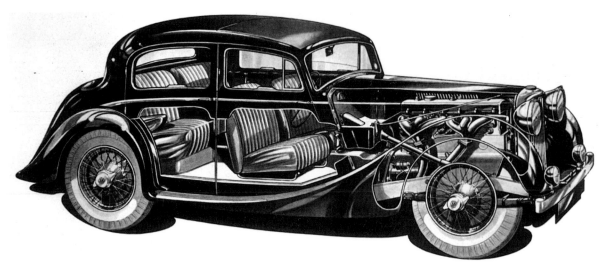

Cut-away drawing of the first car to carry the Jaguar name, the 2.5-litre saloon. This very detailed drawing was used in the contemporary brochure for the model and shows the detail work to the interior, typical of Lyons and all Jaguars to this day.

in 12 months a record 5,000 cars left the Foleshill factory to find new owners worldwide.

Probably spurred on by the problems with the all-steel body and the need to be independent, Lyons seized the opportunity to purchase Motor Panels (Coventry) Ltd, based on the same estate. They already supplied SS with some parts, and Lyons felt that the acquisition would bring him further autonomy from outside suppliers.

All seemed rosy for William Lyons and SS Cars Limited in the late 1930s but there were two matters to consider. Firstly, out of a total of 2 million cars on British roads in 1939, 90 percent came from six major manufacturers: Austin, Morris, Ford, Vauxhall, the Rootes Group and Standard, so SS were still very small in comparison and very vulnerable. Secondly, war was looming in Europe, which would have a dramatic effect on the company, Coventry and the country.

List of Models Produced at Foleshill – pre-World War Two

Austin Seven Swallow two-seater	1928 to 1932
Austin Seven Swallow saloon	1928 to 1932
Fiat 509A Swallow saloon	1929 to 1930
Standard Nine Swallow saloon	1930 to 1932
Swift 10 Swallow saloon	1930 to 1931
Standard Sixteen Swallow saloon	1931 to 1932
Wolseley Hornet Swallow two-seater	1931 to 1932
Wolseley Hornet Swallow four-seater	1931 to 1932
Wolseley Hornet Swallow Special	1932 to 1933
SS1 Coupé (2-litre/2.5-litre)	1932 to 1933
SS2 Coupé (1-litre)	1932 to 1933
SS1 Coupé Saloon/Tourer (2.1/2.6-litre)	1933 to 1936
SS2 Coupé/Saloon (1.3/1.6-litre)	1934 to 1936
SS2 Tourer	1934 to 1936
SS1 Airline	1935 to 1936
SS1 Drophead Coupé	1935 to 1936
SS90 Sports	1935
SS Jaguar 1.5-litre saloon	1936 to 1937
SS Jaguar 2.5-litre saloon	1936 to 1937
SS Jaguar 100 Sports (2.5-litre)	1936 to 1940
SS Jaguar 100 Sports (3.5-litre)	1938 to 1940
SS Jaguar (1.75/2.5/3.5-litre ohv) saloons	1938 to 1940
SS Jaguar Drophead Coupé	1938 to 1940

Chapter Four

Set-Aside for the War Effort – 1939 to 1945

THE likely outbreak of World War Two had caused William Lyons some concerns at SS. In the late 1930s he had expanded the premises, not least with a new development on the Whitmore Park Estate, which doubled production space. However, he had also taken out a substantial overdraft, purchased another company, Motor Panels Ltd, and experienced major difficulties in the transformation of body building methods, all of which led the company into a vulnerable position, which would not be improved by the outbreak of war.

Even before the war actually began an architect was appointed to review the Foleshill premises and to liaise with the then new Air Raid Precautions (ARP) wardens to make all the changes and modifications necessary in the event of war. When war did break out there were concerns over staffing issues. Some employees went to fight. Others were needed for Territorial Army duties, which also meant time required for training. SS had to allow them the time off to train and the company also had to make up the difference in pay between what the army would contribute and what they would normally earn at SS.

When the war eventually came there was an enforced move away from private vehicle manufacture. Production quickly slowed to a trickle (25 cars per week), to fulfil the small number of outstanding orders and to use up work in progress. A last-minute, unexpected order from Henly's for 500 1.5-litre SS Jaguars resulted in Lyons having to write to the government department responsible at the time asking for permission to fulfil this order, which they duly granted. Then remaining stocks of cars were sold off to a local organisation to help pay off the overdraft. At the same time the service department was closed down and the responsibility for that area went out to the SS dealerships. Sidecar production was also initially hit, although this side of the business would prosper later with a heavy workload specifically for the war effort.

A great deal of work was done in preparation for SS's first war contract, the part-manufacture of a new Manchester bomber, including the erection of new buildings on the site. However, the whole project was then cancelled by the War Office, a major blow to SS, which had little other work to fill the gap at that time. Fortunately, during 1940 new business for the war effort did arrive to take its place.

Firstly, the sidecar division received a substantial order for military sidecars, a contract that would see this part of the company through to its sale after the war. Then SS received contracts for the repair and refurbishment of Whitley bombers, the planes that had to do the work of the previously planned Manchesters. Then, after an agreement with Armstrong-Siddeley, SS were significantly involved in the manufacture of Cheetah radial aero engines, although this project was slow to get underway due to problems with the supply of drawings from their old ally Standard. For this and other work more factory space was needed and, on behalf of SS, an old shoe factory was commandeered near Leicester and some of the SS workers were transferred to this site during the war period.

The exacting standards required for the repair of aircraft meant that work took longer than expected, but as a tribute to the work carried out by the staff at SS, more

Example of a pre-fabricated sidecar produced for the armed forces. A basic wooden structure was designed for ease of assembly and lightness.

Mainstream army sidecars lined up ready for dispatch in Swallow Road at Foleshill. In total over 10,000 were produced during the war in khaki colours. Note the somewhat modern curved approach to the windscreen.

Refurbishment of Whitley bombers and their adaptation to take larger bombs during the war. The large wingspan must have caused some problems as the wings only just clear the roof supports in the 'sheds' used by SS on the Foleshill site.

Tachbrook aerodrome was made available for SS to test their refurbished Whitley bombers. Even during the war William Lyons took every opportunity to publicise the connection with his cars, hence this picture of a Whitley alongside an SS Jaguar saloon.

work appeared, leading to the actual production of parts for many different types of plane. Another move forward in SS's support for the war effort was the granting of facilities at nearby Tachbrook aerodrome, where SS became responsible for the testing of the planes they refurbished.

Many of the specialist motor car workers at the factory were moved to other duties outside the company, although some were able to return to their pre-war jobs afterwards. For Lyons and SS it was a trying time, not least because the company made a loss in 1940 for the first time in its history. However, as war work progressed, this turned into profit once more.

Although much of the control of the day-to-day business was still in the hands of William Lyons, ultimate decisions about the work that SS was given and carried out, methods of working, accountability and so on all came down from the various departments of war in the Government. The Government even dictated the amount of pay workers could earn.

Despite this level of control, SS started an Employees War Fund in 1940, which was based on a unanimous agreement with the workforce. The principle was to raise money for distribution on a regular basis to those in most need during the trying times of war. Each employee would contribute 1d for every £1 earned each week to the fund, and the company would match that contribution. A committee was set up to manage and dispense the fund, from which a fixed amount would be distributed to families in need on a regular basis. A total of £35,716 was raised, which was distributed to a total of 618 staff members, with 298 dependents also benefiting.

At a board meeting in 1942 consideration was given to setting up an employees pension scheme, further proving Lyons's commitment to his workforce, despite the war. This finally came into being in 1943 through the Commercial Union Assurance Company. In the same year an independent subscription scheme to Warwickshire Hospital was set up, into which SS contributed 3–4d per week per employee. This equated to something like 25 percent of the total contributions paid into the Hospital Saturday Fund by the workforce. If further proof were needed of Lyons's commitment to staff, in 1943 he also agreed to pay the sum of 100 guineas to BEN, the motor and cycle trades beneficial fund, an organisation that Jaguar still supports to this day.

An interesting period picture of an SS Jaguar saloon in war 'condition', alongside a fighter plane.

A frantic state of work developed at Foleshill during the middle of the war as SS got involved in the production of many different parts for the Stirling and Lancaster bombers, Mosquito fighter and even the Spitfire. The latter was perhaps a little ironic, since only a few miles away in Castle Bromwich, one of the major Spitfire assembly factories would later become part of Jaguar, and it still is to this day.

An unusual order fulfilled by SS was the production of these mule trailers in light aluminium construction with canvas bags.

SS also built lots of minor items for the war effort, everything in fact from ammunition boxes to lorry canopies, mule carts and de-icing tanks. More notable were over 10,000 military specification sidecars, 30,000 amphibious trailers and nearly 16,000 very lightweight trailers for airborne use.

SS also got involved in designing and building two prototype lightweight vehicles, the principle being that they could be parachuted from aircraft. The first known, called the VA, used a JAP motorcycle engine at the rear and the second, called the VB, a Ford side-valve car engine. Neither came to production due to a change of war priorities. The idea of a collapsible fabric sidecar went the same way. Money was still very tight and in 1943 Lyons agreed to sell Motor Panels Ltd to Rubery Owen Ltd to help reduce the significant company overdraft.

When it came to the Government deciding who should build the new Meteor III jet fighter aircraft, initially it was understood that Standard would be producing the entire

SS were commissioned by the War Office to come up with a lightweight jeep and this, the VB, was the prototype using a Ford side-valve engine. The concept never entered production due to the cheap availability of the American Jeep vehicle.

Another concept was the VA, a very lightweight vehicle that could be parachuted from aircraft. The ill-fated project used a JAP motorcycle engine but again never entered production.

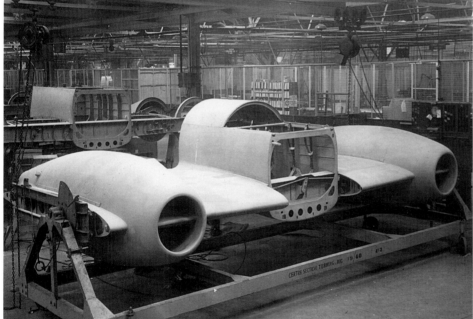

An example of the Meteor III aircraft fuselage, part of a very short-term contract engaged in by SS.

centre section of the plane. However, William Lyons and SS grabbed the contract early on, and although only 98 were actually produced, it must have created quite a stir and been a very positive step for the workforce at the time.

It is a well-known fact that Coventry suffered significantly from bombardments during the war, and the city centre was devastated along with many of the surrounding industrial areas. The SS factory in Foleshill, however, escaped most of the trouble, suffering only an incendiary bomb on one night and a more significant blast on another.

Fire-watching was an important part of unpaid voluntary work that everyone had to commit to during the war and the managers and directors of SS Cars Ltd were no

exception. Each person became part of a team and gave up a night's sleep once a week looking for incendiary bombs, raising alarms and doing whatever else was necessary to minimise damage and injury. The Sunday night fire-watching team at SS was cleverly arranged by William Lyons to include himself along with key engineering personnel Bill Heynes (engineer), Claude Baily (engine designer) and Wally Hassan (a fairly new recruit to Jaguar). Coming 'on duty' at 6pm, after signing on and commencing their 'watch', this team would start to discuss post-war actions, not least the design of new cars and engines, all of which eventually led to the famous XK power unit, the XK120 sports car and the Mark VII saloon of later years.

Everyone worked hard under strenuous conditions at SS during the war, but despite this and Lyons's worries about the company, he did his bit to keep morale up. As well as his wife taking in people who had become homeless, Lyons arranged garden parties in the grounds of their home, Wappenbury Hall, putting on a good spread for the workers and families.

The war took its toll on everyone, but Lyons, SS Cars Ltd and their staff came through it well. The company was back in profit, had learnt a lot from the war, acquired more space and machinery and Lyons was looking forward to the revival of private car production. In 1944 a visit by the Board of Trade was made to the SS factory in Foleshill with a view to agreeing the commencement of post-war work. They subsequently decided that preparation work could commence on the basis that it did not interfere with other duties of national importance. Further to this, in April the Board gave permission for SS Cars Ltd to adopt the new title of Jaguar Cars Limited, resurrecting Lyons's pre-war idea to concentrate on the Jaguar name. By this time the SS insignia carried a very different meaning, so his decision was fortuitous. The change, however, would not take effect until after the war had ended.

A further change that came about after the end of the war was that the Swallow Coachbuilding (1935) business was sold off to the Helliwell Group. They continued to build sidecars for some time, but eventually sold the business on again to Tube Investments. As an aside, the Swallow company name still lives on in the West Midlands under the Watsonian banner, where sidecars are still produced.

So, SS Cars Ltd and Coventry had survived the war. William Lyons and the new Jaguar Cars Ltd had set their stall out for post-war car production and exciting times lay ahead for the business, the workforce and Coventry.

There was a massive influx of female labour during the war, as so many men were called up for active duty. SS took on a substantial number of women to carry out all sorts of work, from riveting to welding, cleaning to painting.

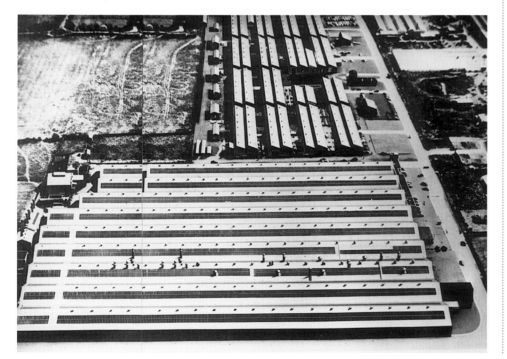

The Swallow Road site after redevelopment of the SS factory, showing the substantial new buildings in the foreground. These were initially erected and part-equipped in readiness for the building of a new bomber aircraft for the war effort. When that bomber was cancelled the buildings were used for the refurbishment of Whitley bombers and later proved ideal for an enhanced assembly area for Jaguar cars after the war. Swallow Road itself is to the right of the picture.

Foleshill Production during World War Two

Whitley bomber parts
Meteor III complete centre sections
Short Stirling parts
Mosquito parts
Spitfire parts
Lancaster parts
Cheetah radial engine parts
Aircraft gun-control parts
Aircraft de-icing tanks
Fireproofed Oxford Airspeed tanks
Amphibious trailers
Airborne trailers
Light scout trucks
Wooden trailers
Mule carts
Sidecars
Lorry canopy sets
Jeep-style vehicle prototypes

Service Work
Whitley Bomber Repair and Modification
Cheetah Aero-engine Reconditioning

Chapter Five

Post-War Revival and the Move to Browns Lane – 1946 to 1951

WITH the war over, everybody and everything needed time to get back to some normality of life. Unfortunately British industry didn't have that time, as the country was virtually bankrupt and the new buzz words were 'export or die'. It was vital for industry to export its goods to bring valuable pounds back into the country to pay off world debts. Sir Stafford Cripps, head of the Board of Trade, insisted that a minimum of 50 percent of all motor car output had to be exported in order to guarantee the supply of the vital raw materials from which to build the cars.

The motor industry was a particularly important part of this export drive and not long after the cessation of hostilities the motoring media were reviewing SS's (or Jaguar's, as we should call it now) ability to survive. Pre-war the company had been able to sell nearly all its production on the home market, and it didn't even offer left-hand drive examples. In fact less than 10 percent of all cars produced in the last years before the war were for export. There was, therefore, much work to do, particularly as the availability of rare materials from which to make the cars was solely dependent on the ability to export.

The revised models for the post-war period amounted to the same mix of 1.75-litre, 2.5-litre and 3.5-litre saloons, now sporting the Jaguar name instead of SS. The smart drophead coupés did not get into production until 1947 and the SS 100 sports car never re-emerged after the war.

Due to the fortuitous purchase of the

Workers coming off shift at Jaguar after the war, exiting from Swallow Road into Holbrook Lane. By now the Jaguar sign dominated the view. Note the lack of motor cars owned by the employees.

tooling from Standard for their engines, Jaguar were now building their own six-cylinder units based on the pre-war design, another of William Lyons's moves towards autonomy. He also negotiated a new agreement with Standard for the supply of 6,000 1.75-litre four-cylinder engines for post-war sales. These would be the very last engines purchased from Standard and the last four-cylinder production cars made by Jaguar, even to this day.

Demand for cars was exceptionally strong, but with the need to export most of production, anticipated buyers in the UK were to be bitterly disappointed. Pre-war models were fetching higher prices than new cars, if they could be found, and there was good work to be had in the recommissioning of cars laid up during the war or otherwise neglected over that period. Since there was initially no service department at Jaguar, some of this work was handed over to the dealerships, which helped them survive during those difficult times, until Jaguar reinstated a specific service department in 1946.

Lyons needed to concentrate on creating export markets for his cars if the company was to survive, which resulted in visits to various parts of the world to appoint distributors. He focussed particularly on the US, which he realised would become the most lucrative area of growth for Jaguar. Cars began to be made in left-hand drive form as well, and the first cars left Foleshill for the US in 1947.

Export or Die – that was the motto for the British motor industry after World War Two. Here examples of the saloons are depicted waiting to board the SS Queen Elizabeth.

1948 and these 1.75-litre Jaguar saloons are in the finishing department. Note the number of female workers doing the cleaning and polishing as the foreman looks on.

There was a lengthy 'demob' period while workers who had been pulled away from SS onto other war duties returned, although some, inevitably, never did, and new recruits were required to replace them. Among new people joining Jaguar was one major influence, F.R.W. England (or 'Lofty', as he became known because of his height). An ex-Lancaster bomber pilot, he had tremendous experience with many motor manufacturers including Daimler and had been a racing mechanic. He joined the company in September 1946 as service manager, enabling Jaguar to reinstate the service department and tap into a good additional source of income.

During the war the movement of labour into and out of different industries had led to an increase in the number of female workers at SS, many of whom remained with Jaguar post-war. They had carried out the 'men's' work admirably, but as many men returned after the war, their duties changed to involve sewing in the trim department, the cleaning and preparation of new cars and some assembly work, particularly when it involved working in confined areas where nimble hands were required!

However, the return to normality was not all smooth sailing. Major national strikes affecting the coal industry and other producers of raw materials had an effect on the motor industry and other manufacturing concerns. Minor disputes at Foleshill were also dogging Jaguar production, and because of this a mass meeting was called in the autumn of 1946. Although the meeting was effectively run by the management and unions, William Lyons took time out to talk to the workforce on the issues, something he would do regularly throughout his life, and a question-and-answer session followed to clear the air. Topics such as piece-work and the newfangled idea of a 40-hour week came up; the former Lyons was already committed to, but the latter would not make any headway at Jaguar, or at other companies for that matter, for some time to come. There was even a request from one shop-floor operative that workers should attend board meetings, something that William Lyons could not understand. He said: 'I can't help wondering what he thinks takes place at board meetings – it is not in the meetings that things affecting the workers are decided but in the factory itself by the executives of the staff responsible for the buying, pricing and progression of production.' A committee of 25 shop stewards was set up to deal with matters and they met every Wednesday. Problems that could not be resolved were taken directly to William Lyons, who regularly made it quite clear that hard work was vital if the company was going to succeed. However, minor irritations and disputes continued for many years.

Before the war and for some time afterwards the company was not totally unionised, although Lyons had come to realise that the unions were a permanent feature of factory life. He tolerated them, but dictated a policy that remained with him for most of his working days. Negotiations would never be considered when workers had laid down their tools. If they went back to work he would talk and negotiate. It was a good strategy that worked most of the time.

Ernest Rankin remained with the company and helped to set up an in-house magazine, the Jaguar Journal, the first issue of which was dated October 1946. Meant to form a link between the management and employees, the first copy of 16 pages in length devoted over five pages to the mass meeting described above, and William Lyons dominated the editorial, writing at length on aspects of what he called 'unconstitutional stoppages'. Half the magazine, however, was devoted to social issues, among which was an employee profile. The first employee to feature was Harry Teather, who at the time was the second longest-serving member of staff. The Jaguar Journal quickly became an important vehicle for communications, but in September 1947 it was temporarily relegated to a bi-monthly publication because of pressure of work. However, by popular demand, it returned to monthly issues two months later.

Lyons was aiming for a production rate of 150 cars a week (the first 100 bodies produced in a week of five working days was celebrated in 1946) and in order to help achieve this target he set up a Joint Production Committee made up of managers and workers, not only to iron out problems, but also to look at new ideas from the workforce on improving methods in the factory.

The winter of 1946–47 saw the worst weather conditions in the UK for over 50 years, leading to tremendous shortages of raw materials. During this time Jaguar experienced their first major fire in the Foleshill premises which started in the spares department. Although production was only hit momentarily, there was a time when the power supply was off during the coldest part of the winter and to counteract this Lyons arranged for hot drinks to be supplied to all staff during the working day.

Many conflicts arose about the quality of workmanship and the presentation of cars. Numerous complaints were received from distributors about the cars and William Lyons himself used to take cars home for evaluation, reporting back on faults. Despite representations to the workforce the situation did not improve over a period of months, leading to the placing of notices around the factory emphasising the importance of quality control. Lyons even used the *Jaguar Journal* as a means of communicating the importance of the issue to the workforce, indicating that poor workmanship may well have been half-expected during the war when everything was in short supply, but that the post-war buying public was not only concerned with the supply of goods, but also with the quality of those goods. Perhaps the Jaguar workforce could not be held totally responsible for the company's position: the country had come through the worst war it had ever experienced, morale was low, it was a bad winter and there was little to laugh about as Britain tried to rebuild itself.

Looking to the future, it became clear that there was a need to develop the workforce. Jaguar announced the formation of an apprentice scheme affiliated to the Coventry Apprentices' Association. Offering formal training and recreational activities, the scheme took on 20 apprentices in the first year, coinciding with the formation of an official Jaguar social club.

By the end of 1947 Jaguar had produced 4,000 cars and over £200,000 had been invested in new plant and machinery. At the time many acquisitions and takeovers were being announced in the motor industry. Triumph had been bought by Standard and Lyons had the opportunity to buy Lagonda, although it eventually went to the David Brown organisation instead, which also purchased Aston Martin.

In early 1948, although it is difficult now to comprehend, shortages were still pretty much the norm despite the fact that the war had been over for more than two years. Indeed, petrol would remain rationed until 1950. Jaguar employees and their families were still receiving regular supplies of food parcels, a scheme initially set up by the Australian distributors Bry-Law Motors of Melbourne. The parcels arrived in Coventry and were taken to the factory by company transport and then distributed to workers by ballot.

At the end of the 1940s much time had to be devoted to the development of new models. The post-war Jaguars were now old hat, and the continued strong demand for the cars was due mainly to the fact that the worldwide supply of all cars was restricted, rather than the reputation of Jaguar for building fine cars.

We have already mentioned the XK engine, which was under initial development during the

Chassis construction for the post-war Jaguar saloons at Foleshill. Petrol tanks can be seen stacked up in the middle. On the far right is the body assembly line. Overalls at this time were certainly not the norm and it was more usual for workers to wear just aprons.

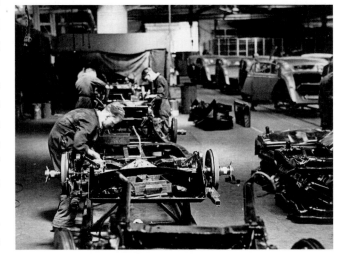

war. Work continued on this project immediately after hostilities ended, and also on the car for which the engine was intended, a brand new luxurious saloon to be called the Mark VII. The project took a great deal of time, not least because for the first time Jaguar was to buy in the complete bodyshell from Pressed Steel in Oxford, ready for painting and assembly. The detail press work needed for such a large car took time to instigate and required a significant financial input of around £250,000 in tooling. The XK engine and the new chassis and suspension were almost ready by the time the initial investment in tooling for the bodyshell was made.

The need for a new model was vital to push the export drive forward. Jaguar decided to launch two models for the first London Motor Show in October 1948. First, utilising a shortened version of the new chassis with independent front suspension and the brilliant XK engine, was the XK120 Super Sports. A stylish two-seater, hand-crafted with an aluminium body, it was never intended for serious mass production, but was rather a showcase for the new engine and a way of encouraging sales until the saloon was ready.

Alongside the XK120 came an interim saloon model called the Mark V. Looking very similar to the pre-war designs it was in fact totally different, utilising the new chassis and suspension but retaining the old push-rod engines of 2.5 and 3.5-litre capacity. With all hydraulic brakes, a revised interior and an all-new steel body with greater

emphasis on curves and chrome, the Mark V was meant to captivate the overseas markets for a couple of years until the Mark VII became available.

Intended to be the export earner for the company, the launch of the Mark V was a very important issue for Jaguar and because of this, Ernest Rankin arranged a launch party and convention for the model at the factory on 30 September. Decked out in

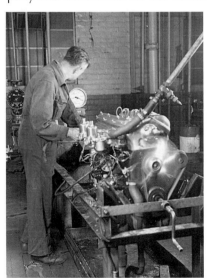

moquette and calico the relatively humble surroundings were turned into a major stage to which the dealers were invited to view the car and talk about the important matters of worldwide sales for this new and exciting model.

Before the convention surroundings were stripped down William Lyons ensured that the workforce would be able to take advantage of this and see the fruits of their labours. As they also viewed the new car he toasted the workforce at 5.30pm that evening. A similar but smaller launch party took place on the Friday before the Motor Show, for the XK120

A very early example of the XK power unit, Jaguar's first in-house designed engine, under test at Foleshill in 1948. This engine initially powered both the XK120 and Mark VII Jaguars and was produced by the company until 1992.

Employees posing with the new Jaguar XK120 sports car alongside the Mark V saloon. Picture taken at Foleshill.

The star of the show: the launch of the Mark V saloon in 1948 in the form of a convention held in one of the factory units at Foleshill, specially decked out by the employees. After 500 guests were wined and dined and able to view the car, it was the turn of the employees to see the fruits of their labours.

Super Sports, at the Grosvenor House Hotel in London.

Both cars did well in developing exports but the XK120 was a runaway success. Embarrassingly, sales quickly reached a level where Jaguar had no hope of manufacturing enough cars to meet the demand. The situation echoed pre-war days, when demand was high for the SS Jaguar saloon. However, after the first 240 cars had

been made, Lyons made changes and bent the workforce to serious production. By 1950 out had gone the hand-made aluminium body panels, to be replaced by all-steel bodies. From then on it was possible to build the XK120 on the same assembly line as the Mark V saloon, which also led to the introduction of a further two variants of the XK120, in 1951 and 1953.

Jaguar workers had regularly enjoyed a Christmas function put on by the company, and after the war this was reinstated. It was held at the Rialto Casino in Coventry, where even management were allowed to let their hair down. It was hoped that this might lead to a closer relationship between managers and the workforce.

The success of the XK120 Super Sports in sales was emulated by its success in races and rallies. Many of the workforce went along to spur on the Jaguar team of three cars, painted patriotically red, white and blue, at the inaugural Tourist Trophy Race at Silverstone in Northamptonshire. Jaguar won the race resoundingly.

Taken in 1950, this photograph is of the main assembly shop at Foleshill prior to the introduction of the Mark VII saloon. The building was part of the extensive new facilities built pre-war for the ill-fated Manchester bomber, but was always intended for eventual car production and assembly. Final examples of the Mark V saloon can be seen on the left, and to the right is the much more modern-looking XK120 sports car. Note the lack of free space between the lines and the fact that body assembly is done prior to meeting the chassis. Little care seems to be taken in the storage of painted wings (centre of picture) or in the casual laying of hides across the roof of a painted car on the left.

Although not part of the remit of this publication, it is worth pointing out that in the late 1940s Jaguar initiated their first assembly line outside the UK. New taxation laws affected the export of Jaguars to Belgium and so an assembly line was set up in Brussels in 1948, although it lasted only a couple of years until tax legislation changed matters again. A contingent of Jaguar workers from Coventry went over to the Vanden Plas works in Belgium to supervise the initial assembly of cars. Over the years Jaguars have also been assembled in countries such as Mexico, Ireland, New Zealand and South Africa, although for strategic reasons that had little effect on production in Coventry.

In 1949 Jaguar introduced a bonus scheme for all workers, based on the number of completed cars leaving the factory. This boosted morale somewhat and inevitably increased pay because demand for the cars was still so high, particularly as the Government had announced the devaluation of the pound that year, helping Britain's export drive. Unfortunately, some workers still looked on such schemes as a method of extracting more work without real hard cash on the table. In contrast, one of the union convenors, a Mr P. Bentley, reported that such things were a 'milestone to better times' coinciding with a £2 bonus that week in the pay packets of the body shop operatives for the smooth changeover in producing the Mark V saloon. There was an inevitable

Out with the old. The very last SS Jaguar saloon (later called the Mark IV because the model that replaced it was the Mark V). The date is 23 February 1949 and Mr Hartshorn, the track superintendent, is on the left with a Mr L. Ashby, mounting track foreman.

crossover in production from the pre-war designs to the Mark V model and as such the very last 'old' pre-war designed model left Foleshill on 23 February 1949. At the end of 1949 HRH Prince Edward, the Duke of Kent, visited the Foleshill factory aged 14. In later years he would become a Jaguar owner, and he continues to be so, even to this day.

By 1950 Jaguar had become a force to be reckoned with. Over 80 percent of all production was going abroad, a healthy position to be in when negotiating for raw materials and with parts suppliers. In further recognition of Jaguar's position William Lyons became the president of the SMMT, serving the motor industry. He was also a member of the National Advisory Council to the Motor Industry.

The company was doing well and announced a profit of over £300,000 for the year. There had been more investment in machinery and they even had more cash in the bank. The only major problem on the horizon was a cut in the allotted steel allocations, which resulted in Lyons putting pressure on those in Government who made such decisions. He emphasised the extraordinary gains Jaguar had made in exports, which resulted in him getting the supplies he needed.

The year 1950 saw the final release of the new Mark VII saloon, the car on which everything at Jaguar was to depend. Shown for the first time at the London Motor

New and extensive canteen facilities opened at the Foleshill factory. The waiters and table cloths were probably for the opening and not a regular feature!

The Jaguar Mark VII saloon, introduced in 1950, the first Jaguar to be produced with an all-steel body made and supplied by the Pressed Steel Company. The example here is shown in Broadgate, Coventry, alongside the Lady Godiva statue. In the background is St Michael's Cathedral.

Show in October of that year, it was *Autocar* magazine that dubbed it 'the prima ballerina of the show' and William Lyons himself always had strong affection for the car, such was its importance for the company.

As a further mark of Lyons's respect for his workforce, everyone was invited down to Earls Court to the Motor Show to see the new car and marvel at the public reaction. This meant hiring coaches and even a special train to take them from Coventry for the occasion, and Lyons provided each employee with 10 shillings as spending money. However, Lyons was anxious not to set too firm a precedent, and so made mention in the *Jaguar Journal* that this was a one-off treat that would not be repeated in future years!

In response, A. Brittain, secretary of the Shop Stewards' Committee, publicly thanked Lyons for the gesture through the pages of the *Jaguar Journal*:

> ...The splendid arrangements that were made for the trip in such a short space of time were a great credit to the staff who worked so hard to make it a success and we extend our sincere thanks to them. It just proves that if Jaguar intends to have a go, nothing is impossible. If we can only be assured of this excellent spirit throughout the whole works, then there is no limit to our achievements.

By the time the car was announced in the US over $30 million-worth of orders had been received worldwide, which put Jaguar at the forefront of Britain's export drive again. Another boost to Jaguar's image was the supply of a four-cylinder version of the XK power unit for a single-seater record-breaking car, the MG EX135 driven by Goldie Gardner. In 1948 in Belgium this car achieved a top speed of nearly 180mph. Applications for Jaguar six-cylinder XK engines were numerous over the years and included speed boats, tanks and fire engines. A handful of these engines even went to another car manufacturer, Allard.

Swallow Road to Browns Lane

William Lyons was looking to the future with the success of his new cars and what it meant to the business. Expansion was the key word and he quickly realised the need to increase the size of operations again to meet the anticipated demand for cars, not least to provide storage space for the Mark VII bodies as they arrived from Pressed Steel. Already the business occupied 600,000sq ft at Foleshill and there was ample room to buy more land and expand on the same site.

Lyons initially tried to get planning permission to build on land adjacent to his existing factory but this was not forthcoming. He did consider a move elsewhere and indeed was encouraged to move the business completely away from Coventry to a depressed area in Scotland or Wales. However, Lyons was committed to Coventry and just two miles away from Foleshill was the ideal site, in Allesley, an ex-war factory run by Daimler.

The Shadow Factory Project

In 1936 the Government put a great deal of public money into the building of 'shadow' factories to produce armaments for the impending war. These factories, all in the Midlands, were built up quickly to supply the needs of the war effort and were called 'shadow' because they were built, managed and run by the dominant motor manufacturers in the area, namely Austin, Daimler, Rover, Standard and Rootes, but were to 'shadow' the main aero engine factories. The factories were purpose-built, up and running by the end of 1937 and run by the above companies under the direct control of the Air Ministry. Two of the factories concern us here, both run by Daimler. The No.1 shadow factory was actually at Radford on their own site, and the No.2 factory was built at Browns Lane in Allesley.

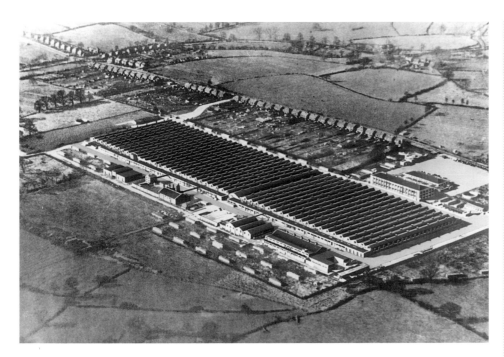

Aerial photograph of the Browns Lane shadow factory, taken in around 1948 before Jaguar occupation. Browns Lane can be seen running across the top of the picture from left to right. The smaller separated buildings at the base of the picture were probably for armaments testing away from the main blocks.

The original principle behind the project was for each shadow factory to make parts for aero engines in large numbers. Then Austin and Bristol would assemble them into complete engines. This in itself was problematic, for if one of the shadow factories was destroyed in a bombing raid it would lead to a shortage of particular parts. So the concept changed so that Daimler and Standard would also produce completed engines between them.

The No.2 shadow factory was built on 62.5 acres of prime land in Allesley and only a week after receipt of the appropriate paperwork, building was underway by Daimler with the erection of the first assembly shop of some 308,200sq ft plus offices, a canteen, test areas and so on. A total production and assembly area was soon increased to 844,936sq ft, with extra facilities for accommodation, allied services and the like. The whole area developed until it was 1,530ft long, 400ft wide and 20ft high, allowing overhead gantries and moving lines to be accommodated. The layout of the factory was planned by the then managing director of Daimler, Mr Hally, and his son. A massive input of new machinery and a worker recruitment drive lead to operations commencing just after the outbreak of the war in 1939.

Initially planned to produce one half of 200 Bristol Hercules aero engine sets, the Browns Lane shadow factory remained in full-time production throughout the entire war. After the Coventry blitz in 1941 over 70 percent of the Daimler Radford factory was affected by bombings and Browns Lane was then also used to produce other products temporarily. It also accommodated many of the personnel from Radford who had become homeless as well as managers who, for a time, did not have office and administrative facilities in Daimler Road.

After the war, with the termination of specialised work for the armed forces, the Browns Lane shadow factory was still under occupation by Daimler along with the

Taken from Browns Lane, this photograph shows the old main gates to the shadow factory in pre-Jaguar days. At this time they sported the Daimler emblem.

General Electric Company and the Post Office. Over time more and more work and staff moved over to Daimler's main factory in Radford, and operatives returned to their pre-war jobs. The site offered excellent buildings and facilities, ideal for car production, with over one million sq ft of space in total.

Lyons made an approach to Sir Archibald Rowland, Permanent Secretary to the Ministry of Supply, about the site and an agreement was made to lease the premises for a period of five years for £30,000. Part of the deal was that Jaguar would help Rover produce Meteor tank engines. It was not until November 1950, via the *Jaguar Journal,* that Lyons announced to the workforce the intention to move all operations to this new site and to sell the existing Foleshill factory, which subsequently went to the Dunlop Rim and Wheel Company, already situated on the Whitmore Park estate. It is worth reproducing here some of William Lyons's editorial, entitled 'The Move to Brown's Lane, Another Milestone in our History' in that issue of the *Jaguar Journal,* as it epitomises his ability to motivate:

> ...The decision is a bold one and the move will not be without its problems. If it is to be accomplished with the minimum of disruption, the utmost co-operation, patience and goodwill will be required of every member of every department in our entire organisation. In other words, the old Jaguar team spirit will once again be called upon to demonstrate that difficulties exist only to be overcome...

He closed with the following comments on 1950 in general:

> ...The year 1950 is now behind us. It has been a year of great achievements in many directions. Our output reached its highest peak and our cars triumphed in one success after another; our export figures were the highest in our history and, closing the year in a blaze of glory, our Mark VII has been acclaimed on every side as the most outstanding of this era.
>
> And now, forward into 1951!

As it was important to affect production as little as possible, the move to Browns Lane had to be well co-ordinated. It was one of the biggest removal jobs ever carried out in the Coventry area up to that time. To keep things under control and manage the move successfully the transfer of one department at a time with machinery, work in progress, materials, and so on, plus the relevant operatives, was carried out at weekends.

Lyons had never relied on outside contractors for work, but on this occasion he entrusted much of the move to a local haulier, Ernest Holmes, who coordinated activities and assembled lorries from all over the West Midlands to complete each section of the move on schedule.

The Jaguar football team during the 1950 and 1951 season, with William Lyons enjoying their success as well.

The machine shop was the first department to make the move and by the autumn of 1951 the tool room and road testing department had also been moved. Coinciding with this Daimler were moving out of Browns Lane, although at a much slower pace. It was a full year before the other departments effected their move, the very last being the paint shop. In all 2,500 lorry loads were used to move machinery and stock to the new factory.

One casualty of the move to Browns Lane was the popular *Jaguar Journal,* which took a turn for the worse when publication ceased in 1951, probably because of the extreme effort required to carry out the move to Browns Lane and the subsequent importance of production. Employees would not see the magazine again until 1960. Also at around the time of the move to Browns Lane, Jaguar formed an alliance with the Manor House Hospital in Coventry, which lasted for many years. Staff could take advantage of a scheme costing on average 1p per week.

During the lead up to the final move to Browns Lane, Lyons, and Jaguar, had to look at another problem – staff mobility. Although the new site was only two miles away from Foleshill, some workers would live closer to the new factory while others would live further away. With 3,000 workers involved in total, discussions took place with the Coventry Corporation over the provision of buses for those who needed them. Ultimately, regular routes were set up involving buses starting and finishing existing routes, as well as some new 'specials' to the Jaguar factory.

On 28 November 1952, to mark the official 100 percent operation of Jaguar Cars Limited at Browns Lane, a convention was organised at the factory. Dealers, distributors, suppliers and the press were able to view the site – Jaguar had a new home. However, the event was not as lavish as the previous convention, and got little coverage in the press.

Disappointing coverage for Lyons of the new factory in Browns Lane. This motor magazine printed a single page of stock photos, with the brief text: '... a huge modern factory at Browns Lane on the outskirts of the City. The work, recently completed, gives some idea of the size of the new works...'

The opening of a new service department at Browns Lane, showing examples of the Mark V and XK120 motor cars. At this time the service department was towards the back of the site, beyond the assembly hall.

Chapter Six

Development, Fire & Expansion – 1952 to 1960

AS THE company moved into 1953, all operations were concentrated on the new factory at Browns Lane in Allesley. The site had become the head office of the company, and it is still at the centre of Jaguar's activities today.

The transition to working at the new factory, although smooth in most respects, was to be roughened by yet more industrial unrest when, just prior to the move, the

National Union of Vehicle Builders called a strike over supposed victimisation of shop stewards. The strike went on for seven weeks, becoming the most serious industrial dispute the company had experienced up to that time. Nearly 1,500 workers were affected, and there was always a possibility that the rest of the workforce could have been brought out too. However, through the Ministry of Supply a joint meeting was arranged to get the men back to work, which they agreed to do, while a more constitutional process finally brought the problems to an end.

Working conditions at Browns Lane, although much better than at Foleshill, were still coloured by aspects of William Lyons's Victorian attitudes. He expected everyone to start work dead on the dot in the morning and not to finish work until their allotted hour. Time to put overalls on to start work or to pack up to go home all supposedly had to come out of workers' 'private' time. Craftsmen were expected to own their own tools and it was not until the mid-1950s that the opportunity arose to join an 'overalls scheme' whereby the workforce contributed a small sum for official overalls which they agreed to keep clean – otherwise most still wore aprons. Breaks in work were another bone of contention. Most work people were allowed a 10 minute break for tea in the morning and just a half-hour lunch-break. The times were stringently observed by bell and the only people allowed to 'mash' tea outside of the allotted times were the 'youths' and material handlers.

The original ballroom and social club area at Browns Lane before the erection of the new office block.

A pensive Sir William Lyons (by this time knighted for his work in the motor industry) looking out from his old office window, which overlooks the entire assembly area with Mark Is and Mark VIIIs in view.

Lyons was also already well known for his factory walkabouts, which at times turned into two complete trips of the works a day. Not knowing exactly when he would appear or if he was away from the factory that day probably led to undue stress for managers and their staff, but from Lyons's point of view it kept everyone on their toes. Once he was 'around' the bush telegraph would start up, informing the different departments that he was on the prowl. Very few of the shop floor workers ever got to speak to William Lyons. Most used to bow their heads and just get on with the job in hand, frightened of his wrath if they were found wanting! Lyons normally communicated through the managers, sending messages down the line about his findings.

By this time the apprenticeship scheme was running well and there was even an apprentices' in-house magazine. Intake was annually, and a group of lads would be selected to learn various trades. To become an apprentice one had to be under the age of 16 when starting work, or be a student apprentice coming in later. Three months after their 16th birthday applicants would pass through to the Apprentices School, where their capabilities would be evaluated. Depending on their aptitude and interest, they would be allotted various training tasks, initially covering the use of hand tools, reading instruments, and so on, followed by specific on-the-job training and, in the case of student apprentices, the opportunity to attend college on a day-release basis.

There were always jobs advertised at 'the Jaguar', and even if you were not eligible for an apprenticeship, you could still get in as a 'youth'. These youths tended to do jobs left over from other aspects of work or more monotonous tasks – anything from making

The attractive art-deco style showroom constructed from the old ballroom within the social club area. This also formed part of the new office complex built on the site in the 1950s.

In 1954 Jaguar's Browns Lane site was opened up to host the Warwickshire hunt.

tea to fetching and carrying and, at best, putting nuts and bolts into brackets. Youths were regularly moved around to meet the demands of the job at the time and the gangers (who used to organise the work and set the work rates) often used to benefit from this cheap labour. They could use two youths to do one job, saving money, which would be shared out to the gang of workers involved. Youths earned in the region of £3 per week, although this was on a piece-rate basis and depended on how hard they worked.

In the factory the Meteor engine contract went ahead, but in real terms less than 35 a week were produced and the contact was finally terminated at the end of 1952. Lyons was happy about this, as expansion of car production was of prime importance. Orders were still flooding in for the Mark VII saloon and sales were being maintained of the XK120 sports car, enhanced by both the launch of another variant, the fixed head coupé, and by Jaguar's fresh flush of success in competition.

Meeting this continued demand for cars created more problems for Jaguar in Coventry. The strike had not helped, but more aggravation was caused by outside suppliers who could not meet the deadlines asked for. As an example, body supply of the Mark VII was not up to expected levels, and there were similar problems with other supplies. This situation, although initially brought about by the demand for the new range of cars, often reoccurred in subsequent years. Although Jaguar was a big earner for the country, in terms of overall numbers of vehicles produced, it was still a very small company compared to the likes of Austin and Morris. In one attempt to ease a supply problem with gearboxes from Moss in Birmingham, Lyons obtained an import licence in 1953 to bring in Borg Warner automatic transmissions from the US. This proved a godsend and the Mark VII became the first model to be so equipped, proving very popular back in the States where customers were used to this form of gear change.

Returning to the subject of the working environment in the 1950s, it was generally considered that to get a job in the motor industry was the best way to earn good money, have a steady job and learn a skill – nowhere more so than in Coventry where there were so many manufacturers and suppliers to choose from. In those days the workforce was more fluid; if someone disliked his job or had a disagreement with management, he could find another similar job the next day without a problem. However, there was a downside to this flexibility that applied to Jaguar perhaps more than many other employers: lay-offs. The shop floor workers were not guaranteed a week's work or a week's pay; instead piece-work was the norm (plus a cost of living allowance) and if there was no work to do, you were simply laid off until there was.

In Jaguar's case, primarily because of irregular supply (mentioned above) and, in some cases, labour disputes, lay-offs were more common than elsewhere. In some cases lay-offs could take effect literally within 15 minutes of the end of a shift. The moment someone was laid off, pay stopped. It was not unusual for men to turn up for work in the morning only to be told to go home and report back the next day, and this could go on for days or even weeks until supply situations or disputes were resolved. An oft-heard comment in Coventry was that if you saw a beautifully tended garden, the man of the house most likely worked at the Jaguar! And this was before the mighty labour disputes of the 1970s. Despite all this people liked working at Jaguar. Most young men in the Coventry area had an ambition to work at Browns Lane. The success of Jaguar on the race track and the imagery of the prestige cars meant something then, as it does today. Most workers could earn more money at other factories, but there was a prestige in working for Jaguar and a camaraderie between the workforce that created something special.

On the social side things were going well. Not only did the factory have a more active social club, but employees were encouraged to get involved in other outside activities in support of the company. For example, the Coventry and North Warwickshire Football Team was sponsored by Jaguar in the 1950s. Another team was formed to compete in the league which was specifically open to Jaguar employees at the time. The Coventry Scratch band was also supported by Jaguar at this point, and would later be renamed the Jaguar band. In 1953 Jaguar Cars Ltd held its first 'Field Day'. This was one great big party for employees and their families, held at Browns Lane, incorporating the above band, inter-departmental competitions, children's entertainment and all manner of sideshows, all sponsored by the factory with some of the proceeds going to charity. One employee from the mounting track made up a little ditty based on his experiences and with good reference to William Lyons 'the Boss' and his continued comments about work:

The Track Song
Now the chaps on the mounting are all sorts and sizes,
There's Geordies and Scotsmen and some from Devizes,
There's a birdie that whistles and Welshmen that sing,
There's lots of us crooners, but only one Bing,
So let's all get together and burst into song,
And keep the track rolling, just rolling along.

Chorus:

Keep the track rolling, rolling along,
Keep the track rolling, then you can't go wrong.
The more you roll off, the better your pay,
Til you'll all roll along in your own Jag some day.

We held a giant meeting it was a real do,
With the Boss there in person, the Works Manager too,
Said the Boss, 'Now look here, we must stop all this rot,
You must turn out more cars, or the firm will go pot,
When prices are fixed, you can earn to the stars,
So long as you're turning out more Jaguars.'

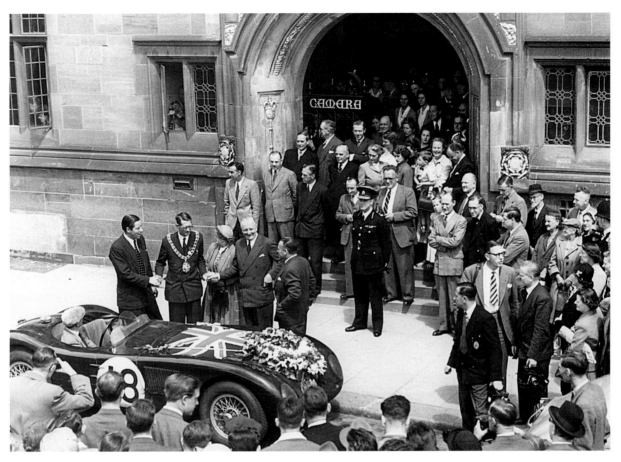

Our Chargehand, the chap with the musical mind,
He's so eager to help, if he sees us behind,
He'll tom, tom, tom, tom, as he carries out things,
We think he's an angel without any wings.
Now he's learning the harp, so those wings he may sprout,
Then he'll plonk, plink, plonk, plonk, as he helps us all out.

To meet the ever increasing demands of the worldwide network of distributors and dealers, a service school was set up at Browns Lane to train dealer staff, a department that became increasingly more important as export sales grew.

The 1950s were great years for Jaguar in competition. After launching their C-type sports/racing car in 1951 it was instantly successful, but 1953 was to be a particularly memorable year, with a resounding victory at Le Mans in France, taking 1st, 2nd, 4th and 9th positions. Upon their return to Coventry, Jaguar were given the Freedom of the City and the winning cars were paraded through the city to a civic reception with the Lord Mayor before making a ceremonial entry into the Browns Lane factory to be met by *all* the employees. It was a memorable time for everyone at Jaguar, a racing victory that the company would revel in for many years and, not least, an achievement that kept sales of Jaguar products rising.

After Jaguar's outstanding success in winning the 1953 Le Mans 24-hour race, the cars were paraded through Coventry, where William Lyons met the Lord Mayor at the Town Hall and a civic reception followed. The C-type Jaguar shown was the one that took first place in the race, driven by Duncan Hamilton, also present standing next to the Lord Mayor.

By the end of 1953 Browns Lane was turning out 250 cars a week and a few months later Lyons was given the opportunity to buy the factory (then still on lease), although this came to nothing. In 1954 William Lyons became the first president of the Motor Industry Research Association and in 1956 the Royal Society of Arts granted him the award of Royal Designer for the Motor Industry.

Never one to rest on his laurels, William Lyons was looking to expand his market share again, this time with a third model; a compact luxury saloon fitting into the range below the flagship Mark VII. It was a much smaller car offering better accommodation than the strictly two-seater XK sports. The 2.4-litre model, as it became known, was Jaguar's most expensive project up to that time. It was their first model to use a monocoque (chassisless) construction bodyshell, and was fitted with a new short-stroke version of the XK engine, producing a quite modest 112bhp. Lyons had cleverly identified a new market for such a car, a notch above the contemporary Ford Zephyrs and Vauxhall Crestas of the period, an easy match for the little Daimler Conquest in terms of performance, handling and price and out-matching other competition such as the Armstrong-Siddeley 236 and Riley of the time.

After the formality of the Coventry city reception, the 1953 winning Jaguars ceremoniously entered the Browns Lane factory gates and parked up, to be viewed by the whole workforce. In the right-hand corner of the picture is the Jaguar Scratch band playing them in.

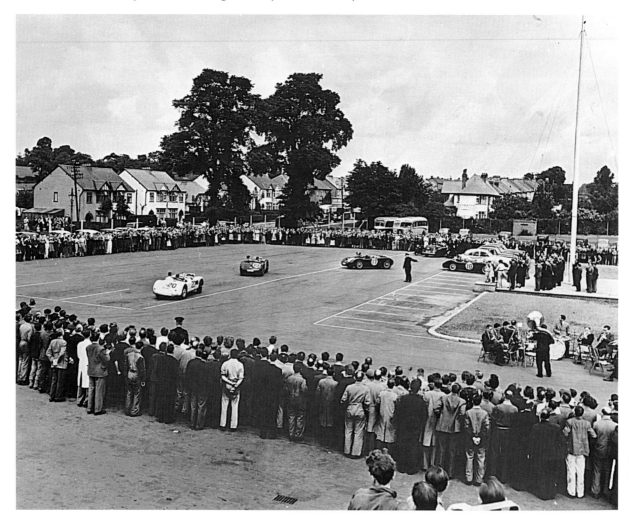

Extensive investment in new plant, a new production line and more staff were all needed for the 2.4 as sales estimates were higher than with any previous model and were easily achieved. Around £360,000 had been invested in body tooling for the new car and a further £300,000 in plant expansion to cope. Staff levels at Browns Lane rose to over 4,000 to meet the demand.

The Jaguar 2.4-litre saloon, arguably the most advanced model the company had produced up to the late 1950s. Introduced towards the end of 1955, it was the first Jaguar of monocoque construction, the body forming the structural strength of the car without a chassis. It utilized a new, smaller configuration of the XK engine and was planned to be the company's most productive model yet.

Although it was not an easy car to bring to production, in fact it happened without any disruption to other aspects of the business. As it turned out, the 2.4 was somewhat over-engineered, despite early examples suffering from minor problems. However, Lyons's belief in the car was justified, and it turned out to be Jaguar's most successful model at the time. It led, eventually, to the Mark 2 version that appeared in 1959, which became one of the most recognised Jaguars of all time.

The previous occupants of Browns Lane were still, at this time, in the throes of moving out, and eventually the GEC building became vacant, into which Jaguar moved its engineering administration. Another change came in the erection of a brand new office complex for Jaguar built facing Browns Lane, in front of the canteen and works social club. An original feature of this area was a ballroom with a curved roof that Lyons retained and subsequently used as a showroom for many years. Lyons had, until this time, used an office within the main assembly building, perched high above the tracks with large windows so that he could see everything that went on. If there was something he didn't like, he would pick up the phone and contact the nearest supervisor, foreman or even manager, make them aware of it and look to see that the problem was rectified. Now, with a new office block, he could move into more luxurious accommodation overlooking the front car park,

At the front of the Browns Lane complex are 2.4-litre saloons awaiting road test. The drivers are affixing their trade plates. Behind the cameraman was the main exit from the plant onto Browns Lane at the time. The car assembly area (painted white in the background) is externally virtually identical today, including the clock. To the left of the cars is the new office block.

Jaguar's imposing new office block overlooking Browns Lane, with the car park in front, used for temporary storage of cars awaiting dispatch. This block incorporated William Lyons's new office, which is the window third from the right.

main entrance and Browns Lane, a position the managing director's office still takes up today.

If all this and the new 2.4 model were not enough, William Lyons was featured in the New Years honours list and became a Knight Bachelor in recognition of his services to the British motor industry and the country's exports. In his own words at the time he said: 'I hope that this honour will be recognised as a tribute to the part played by everyone in our organisation and our suppliers in building up the name of Jaguar...' Production by now was up to 380 cars a week, and Jaguar was the country's greatest dollar earner. Although in some years he was not producing as many cars as other

Union Jacks and bunting being affixed to the outside of the office block at Browns Lane in readiness for the Queen's visit in 1956.

Bottom left: Lyons showing the Queen around the factory. The staff looking on seem very pleased to see Her Majesty and although some of the overalls are not that clean (they would have been working before she arrived), the faces and the hair-dos are immaculate!
Bottom right: The Queen and Duke of Edinburgh being escorted by Lyons to their awaiting car upon leaving Browns Lane.

Coventry manufacturers, he was sending more abroad and, of course, earning a higher price for them. In March Browns Lane received a visit from the Queen and Duke of Edinburgh. They toured the factory and spoke to employees, including the youngest apprentice at the time, one 15-year-old John Deakin.

To temper all this success, the heir to the Jaguar throne, Lyons's son John, was killed in a car accident, and the motor industry was entering a deep recession. Hire purchase deposits rose dramatically, as did purchase tax, which all meant that the export drive was still vital to maintain sales levels. Another problem arose with the workforce as, via the unions, they were pressing for a major pay rise, something that Lyons could not support under the circumstances. Profit margins had been reduced to keep sales up in the US and for the first time production exceeded supply for most models. William Lyons, always a frugal character, was now ever-more intent on reducing costs. All staff were informed and all heads of departments had to look at their overheads and stocks in an effort to reduce both. Lay-offs took place again, storage space at the factory was filled with cars and at one time Lyons even asked the workforce to look at accepting a reduction in piece-work rates to help the company, although this came to nothing. The British motor industry was not in a very good position generally, and towards the end of 1956 Jaguar had to follow other companies in going onto official short time. This

Jaguar's racing success with the specially constructed C-type was emulated with the D-type from 1954 to 1957. This actual car won the 1955 Le Mans race, driven by Ivor Bueb and Mike Hawthorn.

*A personal telegram
from the Queen to
Lyons about the 1953
Le Mans victory.*

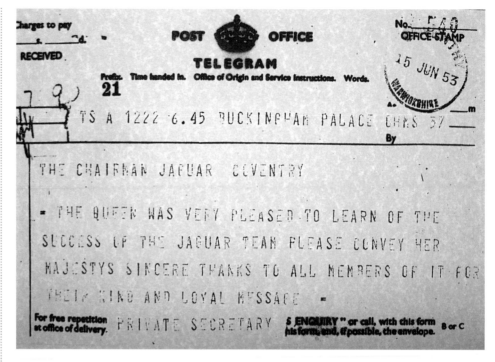

involved another round of lay-offs for selected workers, and the whole factory was
reduced to a four-day working week.

The Great Fire

In 1957 another major set-back to business at Jaguar took place when, on the early
evening of 12 February, a major fire took hold on the factory which resulted in a
temporary stoppage of operations. Residents reported that the blaze could be seen a
couple of miles away in Radford and the following morning employees turned up for
work in the normal way, only to be turned back in droves to await further instructions.

The fire started at the north end of the site and covered an area of some 200,000sq ft
(about 25 percent of the Browns Lane manufacturing and assembly area). The damage
affected the sawmill, the despatch area (which contained several hundred 2.4-litre, XK
sports and Mark VIII saloons), the test department, material stores and some parts of
the assembly line. Fortunately all administration areas, the press shop, tool room,
trimming, paint and other stores areas were left unscathed. Another saviour was the

*Unsalvageable cars like
this rare D-type
sports/racing car and
Mark VIII saloons were
removed to the front of
the factory and later
dismantled and
crushed. The houses in
the background are on
Browns Lane.*

imminent launch of a new model, the
3.4-litre saloon (based on the 2.4). The
first few of these production cars were
stored outside awaiting finishing work.
Luckily they were all moved before they
were caught by the flames like other
production vehicles.

As soon as the fire brigade had
licensed entry to the still smouldering

buildings, Lyons and factory managers quickly put into action a major programme of clearing up. This involved bringing in as many workers as possible to work in shifts throughout the next few nights clearing debris, evaluating the damage and establishing what was needed to recommence operations.

So convinced was Lyons that work could be reinstated quickly that, despite major publicity about the fire locally and nationally, he wrote out to all home and overseas Jaguar distributors and dealers the following day (13 February) to inform them that:

> We are anxious you should know that while it must be some time before full production can be resumed, the work of restoration has commenced and will continue day and night until complete. In the meantime, emergency measures are being taken to replace the facilities we have lost, and with the cooperation of our outside suppliers, we are starting up the reduced assembly lines tomorrow. In no way, of course, will the quality of our cars be affected by the misfortune we have suffered.

Sides of the assembly hall building twisted and collapsed under the heat generated by the fire. This area was to the north of the site and had to be totally rebuilt.

Brave words only a day after the fire had been put out, but thanks to the efforts of the workforce things went well. All apprentices were assigned to the major clear up while skilled workers helped, although many were assigned other duties in preparation for the restart. Of the several hundred cars apparently destroyed by fire, some were salvageable after cleaning and the changing of plastic items such as grille badges, rubber door seals and the like, which had all melted in the heat. Cars which had been totally destroyed were removed to the front of the factory and were finally dismantled and crushed by Jaguar themselves. They had received many calls from local and national scrap dealers wanting to buy up material, but in the end the company announced that it would be disposing of all its own waste by 'crushing every single component from every car damaged to ensure that nothing could ever be illicitly used again.' In the light of the big clean-up operation even Lyons had to stand down on his obsession with piece-work and pay all employees a day rate. The result was the re-establishment of some production on 18 February, and within six weeks full production had been resumed.

Even the Prime Minister, then Harold Macmillan, on behalf of the Government and his party, wrote:

> I am indeed sorry to hear of the disaster which has struck your firm. Jaguar cars have been doing a magnificent job in our battle for exports and it is tragic luck that you have received this blow. But I am confident that with your customary energy and courage you will get production going in a very short time. I am the

The tragic factory fire of February 1957. The massive clear-up is under way, but saloons and sports models were destroyed in the assembly and dispatch areas.

more encouraged in this belief by the accounts of the wonderful work done by your workers in helping to save the most important part of your factory.

The literally hundreds of offers of help came from everywhere: individual Jaguar owners, ex-employees, companies offering storage and supplies on significantly extended terms, and of course there were the many existing suppliers who really helped Jaguar pull through. An example of this was Dunlop, who had purchased the old Foleshill factory from Jaguar in the early 1950s. They not only offered their help but provided valuable space into which some of the Browns Lane departments moved in the interim period – so Jaguar did return briefly to their original Coventry home!

Just some of the Coventry-based companies that helped Jaguar in the aftermath of the fire were:

> Abbey Panels Ltd
> Mortons (Coventry) Ltd
> Webster & Bennett
> Rutherford & Stanton Ltd
> Coventry Gauge & Tool Company
> Coventry Motor Fittings
> Coventry Climax Ltd
> BSA Group
> Daimler Company Ltd
> Carbodies Ltd
> Armstrong-Siddeley
> Lea Francis
> Rootes Group
> Standard Motor Company Ltd

And the list went on. William Lyons even got letters of assistance from the likes of Rolls-Royce and as far afield as Ferrari in Italy.

Moving Ahead

Despite all the upheaval Jaguar was still able to announce its new model, the 3.4-litre version of the compact saloon. However, one model that was not resurrected after the fire was the XKSS, the road-going version of the D-type racing car. Only intended to be built in small numbers anyway, all the monocoques and tooling were lost in the fire after only 16 cars had been produced.

The fire was devastating but fortunately no one was hurt and one good thing came out of it. The publicity surrounding the fire helped to invigorate the market for cars, which led to good demand, particularly from overseas. The factory was able to move off short time and 1957 turned out to be a record year for the company in terms of overall sales.

The fire also presented the opportunity to rebuild part of the Browns Lane factory and expand it to meet the demands anticipated for the future. New buildings totalling 80,000sq ft were approved adjacent to the fire area and the rate at which the new

Although this photograph is not dated, it is retouched to show the proposed redevelopment of the Browns Lane site c.1957. To the bottom right of the picture is the original office complex and in the centre is the main assembly hall. The fire of 1957 affected the foreground area, which is shown rebuilt in this picture. At this time painting was carried out at the back of the site (top left of picture). For orientation Browns Lane is to the right, off the picture.

buildings went up is a tribute to Coventry contractors W.H. Jones & Son Ltd, and testament to the commitment of everyone to the work. The schedule was impressive by any standards:

28 February	Building construction agreed.
1 March	Agreement on construction with architects.
2 March	Steelwork design and construction commenced.
4 March	On-site clearance begun for erection.
6 March	Orders placed for components.
3 April	Erection of steelwork commenced.
18 April	Roofing commenced.
8 June	Roofing completed.
2 July	Final handover to Jaguar, although some occupation had already commenced prior to this date.

This photograph is dated May 1957 and shows production virtually back to normal even if a lot of the old factory has not yet been rebuilt. Mark VIII saloon (later development of the Mark VII models) bodyshells are stored under cover and in front painted chassis await entry into the assembly area.

Taken on 10 January 1958, this picture shows the degree of rebuild work already done after the fire. This is part of the new assembly area and is still used as such today for the XK sports cars and XJ saloons.

Looking over the part-finished assembly area during the rebuild in late 1958. The 'new' area is on the left, while on the right is the original office building, some of which is still occupied today, along with an ultra-modern staff canteen.

The new buildings were used for the assembly of cars, and to avoid the possibility of future fire damage, no flammable materials were used in the construction. New 'ply-glass' panels were used in the roof to provide light but reduce heat gain from the sun, automatic ventilators were fitted that opened if there was a fire and over 1¼ miles of fluorescent lighting was installed.

Despite the fire, the rebuilding and the enormous camaraderie that had built up with the workers, it was not long before more disruption took place with a dispute in the trim shop over pay rates. This resulted in the temporary walk-out of the operatives in that department, which ultimately stopped production of cars. Their eventual return to work cost the company dearly and the protesters got little out of it themselves. Even Jaguar, with all its strengths, was still vulnerable to this type of dispute.

Jaguar was also still at the mercy of outside suppliers and a strike by Pressed Steel workers who produced Jaguar saloon car bodies in Cowley in 1958 dramatically affected the export drive for a few weeks. However, production was pulled back and it appears from the figures that production was made up later in the year, enabling Browns Lane to achieve yet another increase in production that year.

Another move forward for the company came in 1959, when Sir William Lyons finally negotiated a deal to purchase the Browns

The date is 18 April 1957 and Sir William Lyons had addressed the entire workforce about lost profits and the need for everyone to work harder. Most, however, don't seem too concerned!

Lane site for the price of £1.25 million. Although a lot of money, it was important that Jaguar gained total control over its only factory at that time and Lyons's decision was justified when the accounts for 1959 revealed a healthy £2.6 million profit.

The genuine pleasure experienced by William Lyons on the acquisition of 'his' factory was somewhat marred throughout the year by the regular resurfacing of industrial disputes. Early in the year members of one union went on strike over the actions of another union. Then, in the middle of the year, final assembly workers walked out, which resulted in other lay-offs and production coming to a standstill, all for very little tangible reason. There were even disputes between departments and despite raised profits and improved sales it was the workforce that perhaps suffered more than ever in lost wages as most of the factory still ran on piece-work rates.

With many questions still regularly raised by dealers, customers and Lyons about quality control, the decision was taken to set up a quality control scheme to be managed across the board in all departments. This was a high-profile attempt to improve production quality and instil the importance of it in all employees. In one instance Lyons had gigantic banners printed and erected on the assembly lines, reinforcing the importance of quality to jobs. In reality some improvements were made but Jaguar would continue to identify problems in this area for many years. One of the old hands, then in the polishing department, tells the story of how Lyons visited his department one day. He asked where the chrome on brass window frames were for the Paris Motor Show cars. The foreman told him that they were just working on them, to which Lyons replied 'Just working on them! The day that *any* of our window frames are not suitable for a show car is the day I sack you!'

Although quality was an important aspect of Lyons's thinking at any time, he was always obsessed with the cars, new models, upgrades and the future. During these hectic late 1950s years the company had introduced the XK150 sports car (replacing the XK140 from 1957), put a larger 3.8–litre version of the six-cylinder engine into the

The production XK120 roadster outside Lyons's home, Wappenbury Hall, near Leamington Spa.

Mark VIII saloon turning that into the Mark IX, also adding all round disc brakes and power assisted steering and, after the success of the compact saloons (2.4 and 3.4-litre) the company was ready to launch a much improved version in 1959, the Mark 2.

This new model put right a lot of the criticisms levied at the earlier cars. Larger window areas, yet more chrome, a wider rear track, upgraded interior and now no fewer than three models with a 3.8-litre 220bhp version as well as the other two engine sizes. The Mark 2 became the most successful model produced by Jaguar up to 1968. It remained in production until 1967 virtually unaltered, during which time nearly 90,000 were turned out.

Jaguar had successfully pulled through the 1950s despite industrial unrest, recession and fire. At the time of the move to Browns Lane, the company only produced the one saloon, Mark VII and two versions of the XK120, (roadster and fixed head coupé). At the end of 1959 the company model range was made up of:-

XK150 roadster
XK150 drophead coupé
XK150 fixed head coupé
Mark IX saloon
2.4-litre Mark 2 saloon
3.4-litre Mark 2 saloon
3.8-litre Mark 2 saloon

Jaguar production was up to 500 cars a week and there was hope of better industrial relations after a joint meeting with the unions. The major problem on the horizon was, however, lack of space – again.

The most successful model Jaguar were to produce up to 1968 was the Mark 2 saloon introduced in 1959. A direct decsendant of the 2.4-litre model, it now sported a wider choice of engine sizes, more chrome, larger glass area, modernized interior and better handling – an altogether superior package to the previous car. Nearly 90,000 would be produced up to 1967. Here Sir William Lyons, always impeccably dressed, is seen with the car on one of his daily walkabouts in the factory.

Browns Lane Factory Tour – Mid-1950s

SO what was the shop floor at Browns Lane like in those days and how were Jaguars actually put together? Just as today, you could visit the factory and go on a tour. Let's now take a stroll down the assembly line in the mid-1950s. The first thing to note was that most operations were carried out on the one site, from chassis component construction, through trimming, to body painting and final assembly. Bodies and chassis were brought in from outside suppliers but most other work was done in-house. This is not the case today, as you will read later.

The machine shop, where cylinder blocks and heads were produced from solid metal along with most other components needed for engines, suspension and so on, although items such as pistons, shock absorbers and much more were bought in. By this time modern lathes had been installed and one man could operate a series of them. In this case flywheels are being produced.

Left: Still in the machine shop a 3.4-litre XK cylinder block is being machined on one of the new Browns Lane lathes.

Right: Now moving on to the press shop, and although by the mid-fifties all Jaguar saloon bodies were made and supplied by Pressed Steel, smaller components were made in-house in this area.

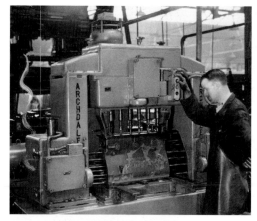

Left: A much larger engine test facility was available at Browns Lane. XK engines are seen here on test and awaiting their turn. Notice the warning signs in the roof area, showing even then the need to consider safety aspects. Every Jaguar engine underwent a three-hour test at 2,000rpm. They were run on what was then termed 'town gas' (remember the gasometers?) instead of petrol because it was cheaper. Then followed tappet adjustment and onto the brake test dynamometer where the engines were run for another hour, under full load at 1,600rpm, followed by 20 minutes at 2,500rpm at half load.

Finally the engine oil was drained and the sump removed for inspection. The engine was thoroughly cleaned, checked for wear and re-oiled ready for chassis fitment. Prepared engines were stored three high in stillages before removal to the assembly line.

Right: Onto the bodies themselves and the body assembly area. Extensive lead loading and the filling of gaps, undulations and dents was carried out using lead solder under heat which was afterwards cleaned and sanded down to a completely smooth surface. This procedure continued for many years, into the early 1970s.

Mark VIII saloon bodies can be seen undergoing preparation for painting. Every body had to be thoroughly cleaned off, de-oxidising it, leaving a phosphate coat onto which the primer paint could key. This was a very messy job as can be seen here.

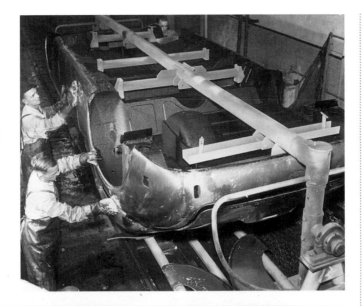

Middle: The bodies then enter the paint shop. At this time all painting was done in-house and Jaguar had invested around £150,000 in a new (although used) paint plant. The procedure for painting was as follows.

A primer coat was applied baked on to 300 degrees. (Baking ovens were gas fired). Then bodies were sprayed with three coats of filler and baked again at 250 degrees. After a thorough rub down, spot sealer was applied to fill in any minor imperfections. This was dried at 120 degrees. Then two coats of cellulose colour were applied, baked at 200 degrees. A further two coats of paint were applied and baked on at 180 degrees. This was finally flattened down to a smooth finish and a 'mist' coat of paint sprayed on.

The picture shows a Mark VII saloon going through the process. Note the lack of facial protection even at this time for operatives. Most other employees were barred from entry into the paint area because of contamination and dust.

The cars were fitted to rotating cradles during painting. This is a 2.4 model and note the ancillary items painted at the same time, such as the spare wheel cover for the boot floor.

At this time and right up into the 1990s, all trim was produced in-house at Browns Lane. Electric cutting machines were introduced and a patented Jaguar marking machine was used on the cloth and there was a strong move towards female operatives in this area. A large department, it may look chaotic, but it was in fact very well organized and completed trim parts were moved over to the assembly areas, in some cases along a cable system above working level.

Bottom left: At this stage we ought to mention the famous Jaguar sawmill, used to prepare all interior woodwork for the cars, of which there has always been a plentiful amount. Specially selected mainly walnut veneer was used, which was separated and then split and matched as seen here before being applied to a wooden base and finished to make up the attractive dashboards and trims used in Jaguars.

Bottom right: Onto the mounting tracks where the bodies finally met the rolling chassis. Here a Mark VIII saloon body is being lowered onto its chassis. Note the fact that even chrome trim has been fitted to the body prior to chassis mounting.

Left: Finished trim was fitted on the trim track, usually to car bodies before mounting onto the chassis at this stage. However, with convertibles, some trimming had to be carried out later, as on this XK150 which is having its hood fitted. In those days extensive use was still made of horse hair which was adhered to the surface, like many other trim pieces, with Dunlop 1356 glue as seen here.

Left: After assembly and road testing, which covered about 25 miles of local roads, cars were sent to the finishing line for touch-up, rectification, polishing and any other minor fitments and adjustments, such as headlight alignment, before moving into the dispatch department. Here, the photograph was taken in around 1954 and shows Mark VIIs and XK120 sports cars awaiting delivery to private individuals, dealers or going for export to other countries.

Right: *In the rebuilt factory after the fire, 2.4 and 3.4-litre Mark VIII saloons flow on the assembly lines.*

The general procedures of production varied little between Jaguar and other manufacturers at the time. Compare these photographs and account with assembly at Browns Lane today, which is depicted at the end of this book.

Bottom: *Extensive stores facilities were provided on site at Browns Lane. Different stores were used for different processes, such as trim, engine, and so on, and much of the parts supply came from outside sources delivered to the factory in batches to maintain a constant supply to the lines. Just in time stock management had not been thought of in those days and in many cases, Jaguar was keen to secure stocks to ensure continuity of production. This picture also illustrates that safety was not at the forefront of all minds in those days – this store-man would today be reprimanded for climbing on boxes!*

Chapter Seven

Empire Building
– 1960 to 1966

A
S WELL as significant investment in new plant and buildings at Browns Lane during the late 1950s, Jaguar was also working on the development of two very important new models. Both the existing XK sports car and Mark IX saloon had their origins in designs conceived in the 1940s, and the compact Mark 2 saloon had shown the way forward, so it was inevitable that two new models had to be put into production as soon as possible.

Much effort was put into both these projects, the E-type sports car and the Mark X saloon. The former was to be heavily based on the 1950s racing success of the marque and would become by far their most successful sports car. It lives on even to today in the minds of most car enthusiasts. The Mark X was to replace the aging Mark VII to IX design and would be built primarily with the US market in mind, giving it a good chance of selling well. Although both cars still utilised the XK six-cylinder engine, other aspects were entirely new, such as the sophisticated independent rear suspension. The Mark X would also carry the dubious accolade of being the widest production car ever built in the UK and the longest car produced at the time with monocoque (chassisless) construction.

Jaguar was already a company with a three-model line-up, but both the new models were intended to increase sales significantly and bring the company extra growth. This would also require an expansion of existing space, for although the Browns Lane site had worked well, it could not cope with the anticipated extra demand. By this time the still relatively new Mark 2 range was accounting for around 450 cars a week. Something urgently needed to be done before the announcement of the new models.

On the social side the *Jaguar Journal* in-house magazine was resurrected in 1960 and the very first editorial came from Sir William Lyons himself, on the issue of unconstitutional stoppages of work – industrial relations still at the forefront! By 1963 over 10,000 copies of the magazine were being distributed to employees. Tours of the

The Mark X saloon under development prior to its launch in October of 1961. Even in the late 1950s Lyons was still designing his cars as he did in the 1930s, with the aid of mock-ups prepared by his trusty carpenters.

Browns Lane factory had never been more popular, and in 1960 over 2,000 people visited the site, from Boy Scouts to university professors.

Strategic Expansion

Planning permission was not going to be granted in Allesley to expand the Browns Lane plant at the time and Lyons was again encouraged to look elsewhere to build a manufacturing facility in another part of the country designated for development. Despite incentives and visits to various places, Lyons looked back to Coventry to provide his requirements and one particular company was of interest.

Daimler, the oldest existing manufacturer of motor cars in the UK, had its base in Radford, just down the road from Browns Lane. Daimler produced its first car in 1896,

Daimler and its owners Birmingham Small Arms were significantly involved in the World War Two campaign. Here the King makes a royal visit to the Radford works to boost morale in 1938, by which time a shadow factory had already been built behind the existing works that would, after the war, be integrated into the main plant.

Aerial view of the giant Daimler Radford factory with the front gates to the bottom centre of the picture and the on-site fire station to the left (still standing today). The specially named cul-de-sac Daimler Road runs horizontally along to the bottom, bordered on one side by the factory and on the other by terraced houses. The railway line runs the whole depth of the factory along the right side of the picture and provided the delivery of parts and transportation of completed vehicles.

an example of which is still owned by Jaguar today. They originally operated from the Motor Mills off Sandy Lane in Coventry, in what was known as 'the largest autocar factory in the world'. The company was bought by the Birmingham Small Arms Company (BSA) in 1910 and two years later built a new site in Radford, which was to become the home of the company until the Jaguar purchase in 1960.

Daimler had built specialist high-quality motor cars and, through BSA, were committed to the supply of military vehicles in both world wars. Government contracts continued into Jaguar ownership, as did other commercial work, particularly the design and building of public service vehicles, for which Coventry City Corporation were one of the largest customers.

Daimler took over the Lanchester Car Company in 1931, enjoyed the royal warrant and was the key supplier of state limousines to King Edward VII, George V and VI and Elizabeth II during the early part of her reign. They supplied most of the royal families around the world and had a significant clientele in places like India, where high-quality bespoke cars were in demand as one maharaja upstaged another. Another significant part of the Daimler business was the Daimler Hire Company, established to supply limousines on demand for everything from private hire to state functions.

Although, in the main, Daimler had been a very successful business, after World War Two it struggled to come to terms with the 'new order'. A significant fall-off in demand for hand-built limousines, coupled with the lack of investment in new models and a general decline in other work, meant that by the late 1950s the company was in serious trouble. BSA were not prepared to bankroll it further, and along came Jaguar at just the right time.

The Radford factory was a purpose-built facility which had been expanded over the years to include the Daimler Shadow Factory No.1 complex, which after the war

Part of the giant assembly hall at Radford. Here Daimler Regency motor cars are being built in the mid-1950s. After the Jaguar takeover this would be switched to engine production, with much of the factory concentrated on bus production.

became part of Standard but later was integrated into the main complex. At this time occupying 56 acres, it was built alongside a railway line used for incoming materials and outgoing vehicles, had an underground complex of tunnels for servicing the on-site facilities (also used for armament storage and air raid shelters during World War Two) and boasted large production areas, even by mass production car factory standards, which were ideal for commercial vehicle assembly. All of this, of course, was perfect for Jaguar's intended expansion.

Jaguar became the sole owners of Daimler on 18 June 1960. A statement was issued that Jaguar, although keen to get the extra production space for its own business, would not abandon the Daimler marque. In fact, Lyons openly said he would expand it. So what did Jaguar inherit from Daimler apart from this factory of one million sq ft, a good reputation for building quality motor cars and poor sales? On the commercial side the bus division had been going downhill, although at the Commercial Motor Show in 1960 all would change with the launch of the Fleetline rear-engined double-decker. Over 50 percent of municipal bus services in the UK used Daimler buses and 90 percent of Coventry City Corporation's fleet would be Daimlers by the end of the decade. The new Fleetline immediately started to sell well and within a couple of years was the dominant force in the PSV market. At its peak over 30 were produced each week at Radford. On the military side Daimler produced the Ferret armoured car, which was successful for many years.

The Daimler SP250 sports car, one of two private cars inherited by Jaguar in 1960. This small glass-fibre bodied sports car was powered by a 2.5-litre V8 engine and it remained in limited production until 1964.

As far as private car production was concerned, this was now reduced to just two models. The first was the ungainly looking SP 250 sports car, hurriedly put into production with a glass fibre body but with a superbly smooth 2.5-litre V8 engine designed specifically for Daimler. This car remained in very low volume production until 1964 and was then dropped. The second car was the newly announced Majestic Major saloon. This was merely a development of the old model utilising a 4.5-litre V8 engine, and it should have been a good seller. It was certainly a strong competitor for Jaguar's own Mark IX saloon, because it handled better and was faster, although its questionable styling was a disadvantage. It too remained in low volume production (sometimes as few as 10 a week), alongside a longer wheelbase limousine version introduced by Jaguar, until 1967. Jaguar and Sir William Lyons had a lot to do to revitalise the Daimler marque, while at the same time making the most of the expanded work space at Radford.

The initial plan was to retain Daimler heavy vehicle and military production at the Radford works but move existing and future Daimler car production to Browns Lane alongside Jaguar models. Daimler's low volumes would not interrupt Jaguar production, but would release space at Radford for another purpose. All machining, engine and axle construction would be moved to Radford. With extra space made a new production line was installed at Browns Lane and a new (or rather secondhand) paint facility was purchased from Mulliner's Body Works and set up. All of this was intended to effect the smooth transition from XK to E-type and Mark IX to Mark X production. At the same time 'kits' of Mark 2 models were shipped to South Africa, where they would be assembled, along with some local production input, and sold in that country to avoid import duties.

In the early days of the takeover there were inevitable redundancies at Daimler, where departments and work were duplicated. All this was sorted out by the end of 1961 and things began to settle down. Jaguar announced an enhanced pension scheme affecting all employees.

Although 1960 was not a memorable year for profits and money in the bank, Jaguar now had a second factory with adequate facilities for the foreseeable future, another car manufacturing name and an opening into heavy and military vehicle production. Times were good at Browns Lane too, because production for the first time exceeded

Jaguar's first new model of the 1960s came in March of 1961, the E-type sports car, here seen in fixed head coupé form. It was one of the most memorable cars ever produced by the company, and remained in production until 1974.

20,000 cars, the vast majority of which were Mark 2 saloons. Also, a further £2 million had been set aside for improving the production facilities in the light of the Daimler acquisition.

However, all was not rosy in another area – industrial relations. Jaguar was still plagued by minor disputes that sometimes had a major effect on production, and various meetings were held throughout 1961 to try to rectify the problems. This was despite the fact that some unions considered Jaguar relationships to be better than many others in the surrounding motor industry. A Joint Shop Stewards Committee agreed to the amalgamation of Jaguar and Daimler facilities, which also meant that only one structure would operate under disputes. It was also confirmed that no stoppages would take place without recourse to domestic procedures and consultation.

The launch of the E-type had been hampered and delayed but finally came in March for the Geneva Motor Show where 2,000 orders were taken. Production was running at full load, something few other manufacturers could say at the time, although the E-type was slow to get established due to the complexities of its design.

Publicity picture of no fewer than seven Commer lorries carrying 28 E-types, the first cars to be exported to the US. They were just some of the 10,500 cars ordered during the Earls Court Motor Show in 1961, worth some £22.5 million. This represented the largest single order ever placed with the company.

From Car Manufacturer to West Midlands Group

Another acquisition was made by Jaguar in 1961, in the form of Guy Motors Limited of Wolverhampton, a long-established commercial vehicle builder. In receivership at the time, Guy cost Jaguar a mere £800,000. With Guy came another established West Midlands company, the Sunbeam Trolleybus Company, which Guy had purchased back in 1947.

Jaguar did its bit for Guy and the 800-plus workforce. Guy had made bus chassis as well as lorries, while Daimler, at various times, had produced commercial vehicles along with military and public service vehicles. The Guy acquisition resulted in the centralisation of bus production at Radford and commercial vehicles in Wolverhampton. Eventually, in 1964, the Guy Big 'J' lorries and tractor units were launched, which would be very successful, remaining in production for 15 years.

Browns Lane became the venue for the next new car launch when on 10 October 1961 a convention was held for the new Mark X saloon. This model also used the new independent rear suspension and its monocoque body was a masterpiece of

This aerial view shows two of Jaguar's acquisitions in the early 1960s, although they were not directly related to Coventry. In the foreground is Guy Motors, manufacturers of lorries and buses, and to the right is part of the Henry Meadows factory, producers of engines, pumps and so on. Both factories were sited in Wolverhampton.

The Mark X saloon, the longest model ever produced by the company and the widest production car ever made in the UK.

The internal use of company products. A Guy Invincible articulated lorry is used to transport Coventry Climax fork-lift trucks. Individual bosses of the group companies also used corporate transport, like Leonard Lee of Coventry Climax who had a Jaguar S-type motor car.

engineering at the time. From the launch and the aftermath of the 1961 motor shows Jaguar received $63 million-worth of orders from the US for this and the E-type, popularity which again caused Lyons to emphasise the need for the workforce to work together if the company was to achieve its aims.

By the end of 1961 the integration of Daimler and Jaguar had been successfully achieved and the first Browns Lane-assembled Daimlers were on their way to new customers. Quality had been improved, some integration of parts between the two model ranges had occurred and in fact more Daimlers were being sold than in the previous couple of years.

On the social scene Jaguar held its biggest-ever Christmas party. It included a pantomime, The Pied Piper of Hamelin, starring Beryl Reid and Ken Dodd, to which over 1,800 children were invited from Jaguar employees' families.

In 1962 Jaguar was granted the royal warrant 'By Appointment to Her Majesty Queen Elizabeth, the Queen Mother' which started to appear on its headed note paper, car brochures and even in the foyer of the office complex at Browns Lane. For many years she had driven a Mark VII saloon that had been upgraded to later specification, a car she would continue to use until the early 1970s.

Sir William Lyons
looking at an array of
vehicles produced by
his Jaguar Group in
the early 1960s. From
bottom right to top
left: Guy Invincible
lorries, Guy double-
decker buses, Jaguar
E-types, Mark 2s and
Mark Xs, a Daimler
SP250 sports car, a
Majestic Major, a
Scout armoured car, a
Daimler coach and
double-decker buses.
At the back is another
Guy lorry.

The combined workforce in Coventry now numbered over 8,000, and although initially there was inevitable rivalry between the two different groups of workers (Daimler and Jaguar), integration began almost immediately. A new social club for the group was built in 1962 at a cost of £35,000 on the old Radford sports field off Middlemarch Road, and it was opened on 20 May by Sir William Lyons himself.

Inter-company competitions were set up that year. All manner of clubs and societies were run within the social calendar of Jaguar/Daimler: everything from football matches and billiards to netball, cricket, angling and photography. There was even a Radford male-voice choir. The integration of Daimler matters into the *Jaguar Journal* also took place. There is no doubt that in those early days some of the old 'Daimler people' were suspicious of Jaguar, the new kid on the block, which, they felt, did not grasp the significance of the Daimler marque. This was particularly in evidence when Sir William Lyons used to visit the plant and make significant recommendations for changes that would have been unheard of to the 'old school'.

The Daimler Long Service Association was 25 years old in 1962 and was a well-supported organisation. At the time 18 staff had worked at Daimler for more than 50 years, 148 for more than 40 years and 198 for over 30 years – an excellent record. This

sparked off the setting up of joint facilities with Jaguar people and a change of name to the Jaguar Long Service Association, which is still in operation today.

The next big news was the launch of yet another car, this time a Daimler. Keeping his promise to continue the Daimler name in car production, Lyons successfully mated the 2.5-litre V8 Daimler engine to the Jaguar Mark 2 bodyshell to create the Daimler 2.5-litre V8 saloon. Much quicker to develop than a new medium-sized car from the ground up, the model subsequently turned out to be the most successful Daimler produced up to that time. It was easily produced on the same assembly line as the Jaguar Mark 2, thus keeping costs down.

On 7 March 1963 came yet another acquisition for the Jaguar Group as Coventry Climax Engines Limited came under their banner. Long term its business had centred around the production of fork-lift trucks, but since 1954 it had also been developing and building superb racing engines for teams like Cooper. It went on to produce world-beating engines for Lotus.

It is not within the remit of this book to cover in detail all the acquisitions made by the Jaguar Group during this period but it is worth mentioning them to show the growth rate of Jaguar, and some of the takeovers did directly affect the Coventry operations. One of the prime reasons for buying Coventry Climax was to get access to their excellent engineering facilities and team, not least one Wally Hassan, who had previously worked for Jaguar in Coventry on the XK power unit. The Coventry Climax

The first new Daimler model under Jaguar ownership, the 2.5-litre V8, which proved very successful. Nearly 13,000 were produced up to 1967.

Jim Clark, Lotus racing driver and world champion, driving one of the Coventry Climax fork-lift trucks for publicity purposes.

After the Coventry Climax takeover Lyons and Jaguar got more involved with the company and its work. Here Colin Chapman, boss of Lotus cars, looks over the new Formula 1 racing engine with his key driver Jim Clark. Leonard Lee (boss of Coventry Climax) is on the left, while on the right is Wally Hassan, chief engineer, who worked for Jaguar in the 1940s.

engineers, along with Daimler and Jaguar's own people, meant that the group had one of the strongest engineering bases in the country.

As an interesting aside which shows the incestuous nature of the motor industry around the Coventry area, after the war Coventry Climax took over part of the old Motor Mills factory that Daimler had originally occupied! Lyons also believed in utilising in-house facilities wherever possible and so, since Coventry Climax produced fork-lift trucks, so these would in future be used in the Browns Lane and Radford plants.

During this period yet another model entered production at Browns Lane, the S-type, a slightly upmarket version of the Mark 2 with modified body and the E-type/Mark X independent rear suspension. It was a perfect example of Lyons's continued ability to launch new models based on existing engineering, keeping the unit cost of cars down, making production easier and creating a further market share.

In 1963 Jaguar introduced a car purchase scheme for employees dependent on their length of service with the company. Up to 15 percent discount could be achieved, which meant that a 2.4-litre Mark 2 would be discounted to around £1,195, but one has to wonder how many employees would have taken advantage of such a

scheme when the average pay was still only around £25 a week in 1962! Two new service schools were also established at Radford that year for teaching dealers and their staff about the two marques.

An important appointment was made in 1963 when Harry Adey, who had started with Jaguar in 1958 as a sheet metal worker and later became a chief shop steward, was appointed industrial relations manager, a job he would retain right through to the Egan era of the 1980s. In hindsight it is doubtful whether this had any effect on industrial relations, as the company subsequently experienced a devastating strike in 1965 when the assembly workers downed tools over payment for door window frame work on the cars. An unofficial strike, it lasted for five weeks, the longest single strike the company had ever experienced up to that time. Since it was unofficial Lyons refused to negotiate before everyone returned to work, and the crisis resulted in Lyons taking out major full-page advertisements in newspapers and a four-pager in the *Coventry Evening Telegraph* on 23 June, to highlight the plight of Jaguar and the British motor industry. The company was accused of breach of a national agreement and within a few weeks the Ministry of Labour got involved to resolve the issue, or at least to get the men back to work. The dispute was finally settled, but not before a significant number of man hours had been lost. The worst losers were the employees, who received no pay during the period.

The Browns Lane factory got busier as production increased and the model range expanded further. In 1964 the Mark X and E-type models had been improved with a 4.2-litre version of the XK engine, better brakes, steering and upgraded interiors. Strikes and other disputes had disrupted profits, and matters outside Jaguar, such as a prolonged gas shortage, had also affected production. However, the extensive range of

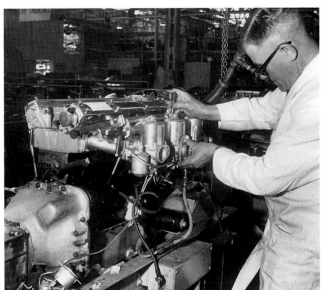

In a small area upstairs at Browns Lane lay the instrument shop, where a workforce of primarily women made up dashboards from the various instruments bought in from the likes of Lucas and Smiths.

Lyons was not averse to making strategic appointments and a chief shop steward, Harry Adey, was appointed to a senior position in the company in an effort to improve industrial relations.

Engines, although assembled at Radford, were also tested with some sub-assemblies added at Browns Lane. Here an E-type engine is being prepared with its usual triple carburretor arrangement.

Our reputation is built on quali

or quality causes hold ups

Poor quality cannot be tolerated

32

33

34

35

36

37

38

39

The assembly line at
Browns Lane in
around 1964 showing
examples of Mark 2 and
Mark Xs in production.
Lyons was very keen on
notices and banners, and
this one 'Our reputation is
built on quality' epitomizes
his approach. Note how little
working space there is and the
debris on the floors.

Mark X production. A body is being lowered onto the transmission. Mounting jigs are now being used because these and all subsequent Jaguar models would be chassisless.

The Radford factory assembly line, photographed in around 1965, showing the build up of Jaguar independent rear suspensions instead of motor cars. This type of rear-axle unit was first seen on the E-type in 1961 and was then used on all cars after the Mark 2 until the introduction of the XJ40 in 1986.

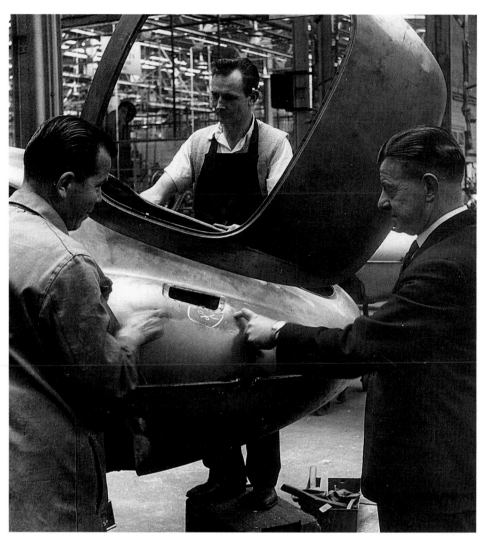

The E-type body was the most complex of any Jaguar car produced and required extensive finishing with lead loading and so on. Complete bonnets have always been made up separately by Abbey Panels in Coventry, which still produces them to this day.

cars produced in Coventry meant record numbers of cars were leaving the plant. At this time the range amounted to:

E-type Series 1 sports car	4.2-litre fhc and roadster
Mark 2 saloons	2.4-litre, 3.4-litre and 3.8-litre models.
Daimler	2.5-litre V8 saloon
S-type saloon	3.4-litre and 3.8-litre models.
Mark X 4.2-litre saloon	saloon and limousine
Daimler Majestic Major	saloon and limousine

These 12 models accounted for over 25,000 cars a year, plus the Radford production of Ferret armoured cars, Daimler Fleetline and Roadliner buses/coaches and the sale of power units to outside manufacturers such as Dennis (for fire engine installation). Then there was production from the other Jaguar Group companies, all of which made the business one of the most active in the Coventry and the West Midlands area, with a total turnover of over £30 million.

Cost-cutting was also at the back of everyone's mind, as it was instilled into all at

Another view of the Mark 2 assembly line showing the use of lines to carry trim above working level – one has to wonder if any ever dropped off and damaged people or cars!

The interior of what has always been called the GEC Block at the rear of the factory. Until the move to Whitley down the road in the late 1980s, all the engineering administration was carried out here. In the photograph are the power train draughtsmen and further down the building were similar departments covering chassis work, electrical, body and so on. To the right is the balcony that ran the entire length of the building, on which William Lyons used to stand to watch the work being done.

Jaguar went on to supply military versions of the XK power unit for the Scorpion tank, produced in Coventry by Alvis.

Jaguar has always tried to be involved with the community in Coventry and in 1961 the department store at Broadgate, Owen Owen, put on a display of a Jaguar engine and leaping mascot in recognition of the quality craftsmen at Jaguar and in the surrounding area.

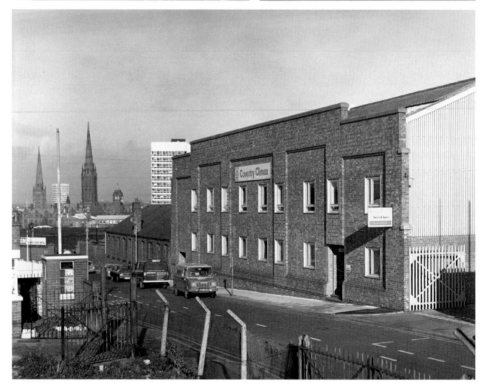

Another 1960s Jaguar acquisition was Coventry Climax in Coventry. The firm was well known for its Formula 1 racing engines and fork-lift trucks – an unusual combination.

Browns Lane by Lyons. This led eventually to the introduction of a suggestions scheme, which was formalised in 1966 with prizes of up to £100 for good ideas that were adopted by the company. In a general effort to reduce overall expenditure, the *Jaguar Journal* suffered again, and publication ceased.

By the end of 1965 development was already well in hand for a couple of new models, a brand new engine and what would turn out to be the company's most significant model up to that time, the XJ6. However, things were about to change dramatically for Jaguar in Coventry and the British motor industry in general.

Chapter Eight

Merger & Mayhem – 1966 to 1983

S IR William Lyons had always strived for independence, both as a company and in the supply of components for his cars, but there had always been problems and during the 1950s and 1960s there had been much contraction of the industry accompanied by amalgamation of resources in an effort to keep costs down and improve efficiency. Although Jaguar had become more independent in many ways after the move to Browns Lane, it had lost some security of supply, particularly in areas like body assembly where complete bodies were now bought in.

There had been much discussion throughout the British motor industry about further consolidation and Lyons, often approached about selling or merging the

Jaguar began using computers early, and by 1966 had built this extensive computer room, run by the very capable Mrs Holloway, seen here on the right of the picture.

business, finally realised that this was the only way forward, prompted by the purchase of his body supplier (Pressed Steel) by the giant British Motor Corporation. BMC was one of the major players in the British motor industry with a 40 percent share of the market. The business now incorporated many of the Coventry and other West Midlands marques including Austin, Morris, Riley, Wolseley and MG, and also had many other parts suppliers under its control, including SU carburettors (another supplier to Jaguar). It therefore made sense for Jaguar to join forces with bigger players to ensure the future expansion and development of the business. As such discussions took place with the BMC boss George Harriman about a merger between the two organisations. The consultations were thorough and mutually agreeable to both parties.

Sir William Lyons with George Harriman, then the boss of the British Motor Corporation.

The matter was kept very quiet among the company directors and the various bodies involved outside. The principle of merging the Jaguar Group with the British Motor Corporation would secure Jaguar's future supply of bodies and other items supplied in those days by companies within the BMC Group. Such a merger would also supply necessary finance to support development of new models and overall make Jaguar a stronger company, providing, that is, that Lyons could retain his autonomy and control 'his' side of the business – something which was agreed upon during negotiations.

On 11 July 1966 the Jaguar board agreed to the merger, the deal amounting to a figure of £18.3 million, and Lyons made a momentous public announcement that would change the face of Jaguar in the future. The merger with the British Motor Corporation would form a new company, British Motor Holdings Limited (BMH). At the time of the merger the Jaguar Group was one of the major employers in Coventry and also still owned other West Midlands based companies. The companies within the Jaguar Group were:

Jaguar Cars Limited
Jaguar Export Sales Limited
Jaguar-Cummins Limited
SS Cars Limited
Daimler Company Limited
Lanchester Motor Company Limited
Daimler Transport Vehicles Limited
Barker & Co (Coachbuilders) Limited
Hooper & Co (Coachbuilders) Limited
Guy Motors Limited
The Sunbeam Trolleybus Company Limited
Coventry Climax Engines Limited
Coventry Climax Electrics Limited
Coventry Diesel Engines Limited
Henry Meadows Limited
Newtherm Oil Burners Limited
Badalini Transmissions Limited
Jaguar Cars Inc.
Jaguar of New York Inc.
Jaguar Daimler Distributors Inc.
Jaguar Cars (Canada) Limited
Coventry Climax Engines (Australia) pty Limited

Although it produced on average 24,000 cars a year, Jaguar was a small part of the BMH team, but it undoubtedly held the most prestige.

Jaguar's suppliers, dealers and employees knew nothing about the merger until the time of the public announcement. There was initially some shock that such a thing could happen, as many of the workforce had developed with the company, always with Lyons at the helm, and it was initially felt that this was the end of a separate Jaguar company and that the moguls of the West Midlands based motor industry would take total control.

This deep concern echoed through the factory. Employees had seen the takeover of Daimler by Jaguar and therefore knew what 'integration' had meant, with later Daimlers being merely badge-engineered Jaguars, and redundancies. Looking to BMC, the business thrived on badge engineering, with examples of Austin, Morris, Riley, Wolseley and even MG sharing 95 percent of components in some models. There had even been collaboration with the likes of Rolls-Royce, which supplied engines for Vanden Plas models, so it was understandable that many on the shop floor at Jaguar were concerned about the future of 'their' company and what it would mean.

In reality, over the course of the next couple of years the workforce saw very little difference in the day to day operation of the business. Some discussions took place about joint parts supply, but as Jaguar's production numbers were not large compared to BMC, this had very little impact, especially as Jaguar always drove a hard bargain with suppliers anyway, on many occasions better than others in the industry (including BMC). Although regular meetings were held between BMC and Jaguar personnel, Jaguar continued production in its own way with further changes to the models to consolidate the range in readiness for a new model.

1966 saw the launch of several new models for Jaguar, and the E-type 2+2 fixed head coupé came out in March of that year. Effectively a stretched version of the E-type, with extra seating in the rear compartment, it extended the market for the sports car and was particularly popular in the US. Thereafter there would always be a 2+2 version of the E-type, right through to the end of production in 1974.

At the UK Motor Show in October 1966 an interim model, the 420, was added to the range, effectively bringing together the frontal styling of the Mark X with the larger 4.2-

Part of a 100-vehicle cavalcade in the Austin factory at Longbridge, Brimingham, put on by the British Motor Holdings Group. Jaguar and Daimler 420s and 420Gs share the front row with Austin Mini and other Jaguar cars and products are intermingled with the massive array of models produced by the group at that time (c.1967).

June 1967 and the Lord Lieutenant of Warwickshire (Lord Willow-Broke) presents the Queen's Award to Industry for Export Achievements to Sir William Lyons. In 20 years Jaguar had exported over 52 percent of their entire production, the highest percentage in the British motor industry. This equated to £41 million of money coming into the country from 126 countries via 134 Jaguar distributors. The US took 49.9 percent of all exports in 1966, while 17 percent went to common market countries.

litre engine mated to the S-type bodyshell, a car that was also launched as the first truly badge-engineered Daimler, called Sovereign. Meant to captivate some buyers who wanted a smaller car than the Mark X, it proved quite successful, in fact selling more than the rather aged Mark 2s at the time.

Just a year later the saloon car range was rationalised, with the 3.8-litre Mark 2 discontinued, followed by the S-type. The smaller-engined Mark 2s were slightly modified and renamed 240 and 340, and similar changes were made to the Daimler V8. The Mark X became the 420G with a slight facelift to the styling. All saloon car prices were strategically reduced to improve sales. Around the same time the E-type had been undergoing further development to meet more stringent safety and emissions regulations in the US. Finally, the last traditional Daimler, the Majestic Major, ceased production.

At this time Jaguar's workforce amounted to 10–12,000 worldwide, and Coventry was producing on average slightly fewer cars by this time than they had in the 1964–65 period, due partly to a credit squeeze. However, by 1967 the Jaguar Coventry plant was on a three-day working week due to a major fall off in demand, some of which was probably due to the aged model range. Important new, technologically advanced, smaller and cheaper to run cars were coming onto the market, and this certainly affected sales of the smaller-engined Jaguar cars – vehicles like the Triumph 2000 and Rover 2000 come to mind.

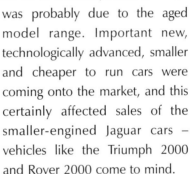

There has always been strong support for Jaguar in Coventry, not least from local businessmen and companies. In 1967 the manager of Coventry City Football Club, Noel Cantwell, took delivery of his new 240 saloon.

From BMH to BL

In reality the Jaguar/BMC merger was more of a paperwork exercise

Well-known 1960s comedian and TV presenter Norman Vaughan takes delivery of his new Daimler 2.5-litre V8 saloon at the Radford factory in 1967.

In 1967 came the retirement of long-time Jaguar man and then vice-chairman of the company Arthur Whittaker. Seen with him here are the other directors from that time, from left to right: John MacMillion (purchasing director), Lou Rossenthal (manufacturing director), Bob Grice (production director), 'Lofty' England (assistant managing director), Leonard Lee (managing director – Coventry Climax), Bill Heynes (engineering director), Arthur Whittaker, Sir William Lyons (chairman), Alan Newsome and Arthur Thurstons (financial director).

with little change at Jaguar but even before the ink had dried on the contacts, there had been backroom discussions on further amalgamations in the British motor industry. Prompted by many things, including poor financial figures for the new group, previous discussions about amalgamating the car industry and financial incentives, the then Minister of Technology, Anthony Wedgwood Benn, encouraged serious talks between the two big players, British Motor Holdings and Leyland. Leyland already owned Standard-Triumph and Rover and had previously discussed mergers with BMC.

The principle of bringing both groups together was based on the thought that a combined British motor industry would be best placed to tackle the onslaught of foreign competition from Europe, the United States and Japan. So it was that on 17 January 1968 an announcement was made that the two groups would merge, although the deal was not ratified until May after much argument about who should do what and whether Leyland should takeover BMH or effect a merger. From all this the British Leyland Motor Corporation (BLMC, or just BL) was born, incorporating most of the British car industry.

BL brought together the majority of the remaining car manufacturers in the UK: Jaguar, Daimler, Rover, Triumph, Vanden Plas, MG, Austin-Healey, Wolseley, Riley and of course, Austin and Morris, as well as commercial vehicle divisions like Leyland, Daimler, Guy, Morris Commercial and the like. As far as cars were concerned, *Autocar* magazine at the time listed 40 models then being produced by the above companies.

Coinciding with the formation of this new group came a major change in Sir William Lyons's position. He announced that he was relinquishing his position as managing director of the Jaguar Group, although he remained chairman and chief executive. To take his place the original Browns Lane service manager and later director, F.R.W 'Lofty' England, and Robert Grice became joint managing directors of Jaguar Cars Limited. Lyons was also made deputy chairman of British Leyland. Sir George Harriman, the big chief at BMH, was forced to resign, and the chairman's position at British Leyland was taken by Sir Donald Stokes (a Leyland man).

The news came as quite a shock to the Jaguar workforce, as once again they had been totally unaware of what had been going on in the background before the announcement was made to them on 19 January. Part of that statement read:

> BMH and Leyland are convinced that the merger is in the best interests of the
> country, their companies and all their employees. Jaguar will be able to pursue
> its own course within the overall policy of the new corporation...

Still recovering from the BMH merger, this statement did at least go some way to allaying the immediate fears of the Coventry workers, and when the combined business became operational in May of that year Jaguar continued to run as it had before. The most important man, Sir William Lyons, was still very much in evidence.

In April the new boss at BL issued a memo informing everyone that the new logo was meant to indicate a spinning wheel, but as far as Jaguar was concerned, it was either called 'the flying arsehole' or resembled 'water down the plug hole', the way the group eventually ended up! The new logo had to be used on all commercial and public service vehicles (including Daimler's) and even appeared eventually on some Jaguar parts such as cylinder heads. It only ever appeared on the exterior of Jaguar and Daimler motor cars where they were assembled abroad or on 'running in' stickers. A prototype form of badge incorporating the BL logo was totally rejected by Jaguar – thankfully – and some workers claimed that they would have refused to fit it on 'their' cars.

A month later Jaguar announced a new car, a vehicle that had been developed during the BMH merger, effectively the first amalgamation of resources, the Daimler DS 420 limousine. A member of the BMH Group of companies, the Vanden Plas Coachworks in London, had been used to create a new prestige limousine design for the carriage trade, ambassadorial work, company chairmen and even royalty. The body was mated to an extended Jaguar Mark X platform, with mechanical aspects also taken from the Jaguar parts bin, not least the XK engine. Trimmed out to the highest standards the DS 420 proved to be an excellent vehicle from which even hearses were produced, and it was a fitting replacement for the existing limousines produced by the group, namely the Vanden Plas (ex-Austin) Princess and the Daimler Majestic Major long wheelbase.

It took some time for British Leyland to make its mark on Browns Lane, with more urgent concerns elsewhere in the group. After some months actions spoke louder than

The British Leyland logo, which resulted in some interesting observations from Jaguar personnel!

*Daimler DS 420
limousines were hand
trimmed, initially in
London, later at
Browns Lane.*

words when the first major changes started to take place affecting Jaguar's dealer network. There then followed many other moves, including the complete upheaval and relocation of some departments to other sites in the group.

The range of models produced at Browns Lane in mid-1968 had been modified and reduced again to:

Jaguar E-type Series 2 sports	fhc/roadster/2+2
Jaguar 420G saloon	rebadged Mark X
Jaguar 420 saloon	
Daimler 420 Sovereign saloon	
Jaguar 240 saloon	rebadged 2.4-litre Mark 2
Daimler V8 250 saloon	rebadged 2.5-litre model

With the eventual announcement of the new XJ6 saloon in September of that year, the above range would be further drastically reduced to just the E-types and, for a short while, the Daimler 420 Sovereign and Jaguar 420G models, both of which would also be gone by 1970.

There was still tremendous rivalry between the different companies. Anyone working for Jaguar considered themselves a Jaguar employee, not a British Leyland employee. This was good for Jaguar's 'family' image, but not so good for a big and cumbersome group like BL, with what would turn out to be ever-spiralling costs and problems.

Despite all this in those early days of BL, Jaguar was able to keep its head above water and on 26 September 1968 announced its most important new model up to that time, a car that had been developed over a long gestation period, the XJ6 saloon. Although very much based on previous technology in that the car used the existing XK

engine (yet again!) and independent rear suspension, a revised and somewhat revolutionary form of front suspension was employed, which together with the very latest in tyre technology courtesy of Dunlop turned the new Jaguar saloon into a world beater. Voted 'Car of the Year' by *Car* magazine in 1969, the model was the embodiment of a principle of a one-model saloon car policy at Browns Lane, a situation that would continue until 1999.

Although always planned by Lyons, the XJ6 also played somewhat into the hands of British Leyland, as they attempted to reduce and rationalise the enormous model range within the group. Because of Browns Lane and the XJ6, plans were dropped for a luxurious new Rover to compete with Jaguar. However, other smaller Jaguar models were also phased out, leaving this area of the business to the likes of Rover and Triumph.

Within a few months the demand for the XJ6 was so great that it just could not be met, as at the time only about 10 cars per week were coming off the line, due mainly to industrial disputes and a shortage of parts from other companies, including some of BL's own. As soon as parts became available again, others would go out of stock. Despite this Jaguar took on over 800 new people to train on assembly and allied duties

The culmination of a significant development period brought about a one-model saloon car policy for Jaguar in 1968 with the announcement of the XJ6 saloon. Still looking very much like a Jaguar, it did lose the usual prominent form of radiator grille and leaping mascot on the bonnet.

to cope with the intended increase in production as soon as parts were available. A night shift was also organised. All these measures were important, as the XJ6 had been geared financially to large production numbers and if this was not achieved, it would lead to major losses for the company and, of course, British Leyland.

Over the course of the next 12 months production of the other 'older' models was dropped and a Daimler Sovereign version of the XJ6 was announced. In the same year (1969) the Leyland Truck and Bus Division started to have an effect on the Jaguar Group. Henry Meadows, along with Guy Motors, was moved over, although Lyons, for a time, remained chairman of Guy.

Industrial relations, particularly outside of Jaguar, were no better. Constant strikes and disputes hampered Jaguar production to the point where there were very few full weeks of production completed in 1970. Demand was still exceptionally high for the XJ6 saloon but Jaguar just could not meet the requirements of sales. The new Industrial Relations Act of 1971, brought into effect by the new Conservative government, would not improve the situation.

Another ongoing development project for Jaguar finally came to fruition with the launch of the V12 engine, only the second engine ever designed and built by the company. A large engine of 5.3-litres capacity producing around 272bhp, it was a prestige unit meant to impress the favoured US market against the home-grown V8s. Announced in 1971, it was first seen in the next version of the E-type sports car, the Series 3, although the XJ saloon was always destined to receive it later in production.

Celebrities and dignitaries were regular visitors to Browns Lane. Here Lofty England is seen with the Duke of Kent and an E-type Series 3. The Duke has always been a strong supporter of Jaguar and continues to own one to this day.

The engine, developed by Jaguar's strong team of engineers including Wally Hassan, Claude Baily and Harry Mundy, was a superb piece of engineering, built alongside the existing XK engine at the old Daimler works in Radford.

Over the course of 1970 and 1971 serious consideration was given to factory expansion, because in spite of disruptions to production in 1971 the company managed to build no fewer than 31,500 cars. Sites were looked at across the road from the existing factory but initially nothing came of this and Lord Stokes of BL was keen for Jaguar to look at an outside development area because of the possible incentives that could be gained from Government.

The year 1972 was to be important and momentous for Jaguar in many

Sir William Lyons celebrated his 70th birthday on 4 September 1971 and the Guild of Motoring Writers presented him with this cake.

ways, not least because it heralded the 50th anniversary of the company in September of that year. It also brought in another expansion in model range, with the final launch of the V12-engined saloons, the Jaguar XJ12 and Daimler Double Six, plus longer wheelbase versions of the bodyshell to improve rear passenger leg room. This was followed by the second collaboration with Vanden Plas, the Daimler Double Six Vanden Plas saloon – the flagship of the range.

The VDP was based on the standard Daimler Double Six which was assembled at Browns Lane, although it was completed without much of the trim and final paint finish. The cars were shipped down to London for VDP finishing, which included fitting a bespoke interior and trim, exterior paintwork, revised chrome detailing and even a vinyl roof covering.

If there was ever a case of bad timing, it was in the launch of the 12-cylinder saloons in 1972, as it coincided with another momentous strike for the company – the worst on record. Production completely stopped for 10 weeks in the middle of the year, an official stoppage, over the transition policy of BL from piece-work to day rates. Eventually this dispute was resolved, although it somewhat over-shadowed the retirement of the founder of the company, Sir William Lyons, who retained his position as honorary president.

Sir William Lyons with his replacement at the top F.R.W. England in the Browns Lane showroom with an E-type Series 3 sports car in the background.

With Lyons's retirement came the appointment of F.R.W. England as the new chairman and chief executive at Jaguar, although he was over 60 years of age at the time. By this time the BL grip on Jaguar was starting to tighten. More controls were put in place, there was a cross-flow of Jaguar people out to other BL companies and other non-Jaguar people moved into Browns Lane. Accountability started to change with, in many cases, administration having to be passed down to other people outside of Browns Lane for final approval. The previously essential 'family atmosphere' at the company faded into oblivion as people continually changed and moved around, never knowing from one day to the next where they would be and what they would be responsible for. Lord Stokes, the then boss of BL, did make a public statement to the effect that Jaguar was a vital part of the ongoing success of British Leyland, but tempered his words with the comments that Jaguar needed BL just as much as BL needed Jaguar!

One distraction from all this was the Queen's Silver Wedding Anniversary, also in 1972. As part of Coventry's celebrations Jaguar was invited to take over the city's art gallery to display its wares and history. Sir William Lyons opened the gallery and the display continued for several months along with many other celebrations marking the anniversary for the company and its involvement with Coventry.

Whether by deliberate action or coincidence, Lyons's retirement meant that BL could now play a more intense roll in the running of Jaguar. In 1973 the chairman, Lofty England, was asked to appoint Geoffrey Robinson (the BL man in charge of the Italian Innocenti company) to the post of managing director, and this took effect in September of that year. Robinson was a likeable character and he did instil some confidence in the workforce through his visits to the shop floor, sometimes during the nightshift, and his major announcement that he planned to continue paying good wages, improving facilities and generating sufficient profits to pay for them. His very ambitious plan was to keep Jaguar autonomous and raise production from 30,000 cars a year to 60,000 within two years – and that was only the start! He anticipated an ongoing investment of over £60 million in Jaguar, although he failed to indicate where it would come from, and this would mean a major expansion of operations at the Browns Lane plant.

Geoffrey Robinson, managing director of Jaguar in 1973.

With what appeared to be a healthy order book (although very much over-stated, as Jaguar dealers never actually got all the cars they wanted), Robinson set about fundamental staffing changes at Browns Lane, removing many of the established managers and supervisors and replacing them with new people. His reasoning was to improve management skills and get away from the dictatorial control over the whole company that one man, Lyons, had established over the years. With these changes came a lot of unrest and uncertainty although Robinson developed a good rapport with the many unions involved. He then started to attack the parts suppliers, which for many years had let Jaguar down, either through lack of supply (because Jaguar was a small cog in the giant wheel of West Midlands car manufacture), or through poor quality. Robinson was to use the benefits of the British Leyland numbers game not only to bring down costs, but also to use their muscle to improve quality and rationalise the needs of Jaguar with those of other makes in the group.

By 1974 a new purchasing director was appointed to achieve this aim, and Mike Beasley was brought in as staff director, with responsibility for production and plant engineering. With a Ford background one of his new jobs was to look after the

Jaguar Directors in 1974 alongside one of the new XJ6 Series 2 saloons. From left to right: Ken Edwards (personnel), J. McGrath (finance), I.R Forster (purchasing), Geoffrey Robinson (chief executive), R. Lindsay (manufacturing), R.J. Knight (engineering) and D.A. Currie (sales).

installation of a new paint plant at Pressed Steel, which Jaguar would take advantage of. He was also responsible for trying to find and improve space on the assembly line area for future expansion. More buildings and facilities were required and an announcement was made that Jaguar wished to purchase and build on green belt land adjacent to the existing factory near Coundon Green. A long and protracted plan evolved which would take effect later.

Jaguar's service department was relocated in 1973 to Kingfield Road in Coventry. The new facility is shown here with examples of one of the early XJ12 saloons, along with a police specification XJ6, 420s, 420Gs and Mark 2s.

However, along the way national problems were to hit Jaguar and all other producers. A major coal dispute reigned for some considerable time and led the Government to implement a three-day working week to conserve fuel supplies. This meant lay-offs, enforced loss of production and money and ultimately affected any investment by the group, as BL's anticipated profits of £68 million in 1973 were reduced to a £16 million loss in just the first half of the financial year.

Despite all this Jaguar's turnover for 1974 had actually increased, with over 14,000 cars being sold in the UK alone, beating the previous two years. Some of this success must be put down to the launch of the Series 2 versions of the XJ saloon car range. By the end of 1974 the last E-types had left the line, as it was struggling to sell after 13 years in production, but Jaguar had been working on its replacement. The new car was not a true sports car, as Jaguar, like most other manufacturers, considered that the old two-seater, wind-in-the-hair style of motoring was dead.

As to Robinson's continuing wild plans for expansion and massive investment, these were to be quickly halted when, at the end of 1974, it became known that BL was virtually broke. The Government had to be called in to effectively take control, leading to a degree of public ownership. Total losses that year amounted to some £24 million, with liabilities of another £35 million, and the banks refused to lend any more money. Unfortunately Jaguar was right in the middle of all this.

After informing the House of Commons of the problem, the then Minister of Trade and Industry, Anthony Wedgwood Benn, decided to commission a major report on British Leyland and its future direction. Sir Don Ryder, later Lord Ryder, the chairman of the National Enterprise Board, was to head up an investigation into the business. The Ryder Report (as it became known) was released in April 1975 and made several important, if later to be found flawed, suggestions that would profoundly affect Jaguar. It recommended that all product planning, styling and engineering development should be centralised in Solihull (at Rover) for *all* future BL models. For Browns Lane this would mean the removal of specialist staff, and leave Jaguar unable to control its own destiny as far as new models was concerned. Even worse, the amalgamation of all the car companies into one profit centre was proposed, effectively signing the death warrant for Jaguar as a separate business and condemning much of the workforce to unemployment as well. The third recommendation contained in the report was that to effect a major improvement in labour relations an employee participation plan was to be set up, with employee representation and consultation over new models, planning, sales, marketing and even financial performance. William Lyons had realised early on that such a scheme would not work, and would only contribute to bureaucracy.

The outcome of all this was a major set-back for Robinson, Jaguar and the workforce. The board of Jaguar Cars was quietly disbanded, the independent name and company were dropped and it became just a section of the conglomerate British Leyland. Finally, Geoffrey Robinson resigned from Jaguar and BL. This left a void at Jaguar and little confidence in the future from the workforce or even the dealerships and motoring media. The irony was that Jaguar was probably the company within BL with the most profit potential, best loyalty and worldwide reputable name. In real terms the Jaguar company might have been able to survive better if it had been sold off, leaving all at British Leyland to fight their own battles for survival.

After the recommendations of the Ryder Report and the Government's input, money was made available for BL and the Government took a major stake in the company under the appropriately named British Leyland Bill (bill being the operative word!). However, there was confusion over where things went from there. The group became known as British Leyland Limited from this time, and one of the four distinct divisions was Leyland Cars (incorporating Jaguar of course). Very few true Jaguar people were appointed to any positions of seniority with this change.

Despite so much unrest at Jaguar during this time they nevertheless brought their next important new model to launch – the XJ-S grand touring car in September 1975. Based on the floorplan of the XJ saloons, utilising the V12 engine, this was a new direction for Jaguar with marketing aimed at a different buyer who was used to the likes of Ferrari, Maserati or even Jensen. The most expensive production car made by Jaguar up to that time, it retailed at £8,900. It was a big gamble that initially did not pay off.

The Jaguar XJ-S, announced in 1975, a total departure stylistically from anything Jaguar had produced before. It has since become an 'evergreen' for the company after 21 years in production

With Jaguar's sales and marketing division now entrenched in the BL camp, for the first time a new Jaguar launch would not take place after a dealer convention at the factory, at a major show or even at a prestigious location – this time it took place at the home of Austin in Longbridge near Birmingham and this, more than anything else up to this time, had a major effect on morale at Browns Lane. The rot had firmly set in as far as they were concerned and more was yet to come.

The next blow to the morale of Jaguar people was just around the corner. The announcement came that British Leyland were going racing, via Warwickshire racing team Ralph Broad, and the car would be a highly modified Jaguar XJ12 coupé. However, no one at Jaguar was ever involved in the project and the prominent name on the side of the blue and white car was, of course, BL and not Jaguar. By the end of 1977 the project had been cancelled after seven races and not a single win, to the humiliation of those associated with the Jaguar name and all at Browns Lane.

With a desperate need for BL to cut costs there were many rumours around, one of which was that Jaguar production might be transferred to Rover's Solihull facility, which was newer, better equipped and had spare capacity. Although this never happened, another major blow to morale came in those early years of numerous changes and confusion when the Jaguar and ex-Daimler plants were split up, to run separately with little connection between them, although one still supplied the other with components. By this time of course all vehicle production had been removed from Radford, which had become part of Leyland Vehicles, leaving the factory to the production and assembly of engines and axles. The factories were even renamed and in the case of Browns Lane, it became simply 'Leyland Cars Large Car Assembly Plant No.2' and Radford became 'Radford Engines and Transmission Plant'.

The most obvious move affecting the workforce morale was the removal of all Jaguar signage from Browns Lane and the change from Jaguar's normal green colour scheme to BLs blue and white. Some people, like Peter Craig (then plant director) and

A glimmer of hope for Jaguar or perhaps a deliberate ploy to hit out at BL. The Jaguar football team celebrating their successes against the British Leyland Bathgate team in the Leyland Cup League in 1975. Alongside the still new XJ-S model team manager David Anderson (by the leaping mascot) is with Peter Craig (manufacturing director) and the rest of the team.

Michael Beasley, instigated the careful storage of anything with the Jaguar name. Everything was logged showing where or who kept it, whether on site or even in workers homes! Obviously they had the foresight to realise that Jaguar would rise again in the future. From then on even to today, Jaguar employees refer to that time as 'Jaguar's blue period'. In 1976 Jaguar even lost its own independent motor show stand in London. Instead its cars were merely displayed alongside other British Leyland products, another bitter blow to the Jaguar 'family' in Coventry.

Peter Craig was one of Jaguar's longest serving employees, having started with SS in 1941 and worked his way up through the ranks, finally becoming plant director in 1973. He was a prime mover in doing anything to retain the Jaguar 'family' at Browns Lane. He, along with then PR man and later authoratitive Jaguar historian Andrew Whyte, instigated the publication of a new in-house magazine, *Jaguar Topics*. With a very tight budget of just £500 an issue (published bi-monthly) and with material gathered on social and company issues, although nothing contentious, the first issue appeared right in the middle of the BL turmoil of January/February 1977. Unfortunately, Peter Craig died prematurely, before he could see the fruits of his labours. His place as boss of Jaguar manufacturing was taken by Mike Beasley, still a major force in Jaguar today.

That first issue of *Jaguar Topics* was a pretty slim newsletter printed in black and white and concentrated on an obituary for Peter Craig, but also set the scene for future content with bits of interest relating to what was happening within Jaguar and on the social scene. It was rightly intended as a boost to the workforce and as a method of communication to keep the 'family feel' alive. The long-lived suggestion scheme got good mention because, even in these times, the top award stood at £1,250, a very tempting amount to encourage interaction of ideas. Elsewhere, the Jaguar social club on the Radford site was boosted by a £45,000 refurbishment and boasted no fewer than 22 societies, covering everything from tenpin bowling to angling, shooting and caravanning.

Despite everything British Leyland could do to 'destroy' Jaguar, a rebellious act came from the engineering director Bob Knight, who fought hard to maintain Jaguar's engineering department separately from BL. He succeeded, was given a CBE in 1977 and later became managing director of Jaguar from 1978 to 1980. Another possible fiasco was narrowly averted when the BL board seriously considered producing all cars under the Leyland name, relegating marque names like Jaguar to merely model names, a return to where it all started for Jaguar in 1935 with the SS Jaguar saloon. Fortunately this aspect of the BL debacle never materialised.

The attitude of Jaguar's Coventry staff was changing. Although the company had always had its conflicts between workers, unions and management, things were never as bad as they were during the British Leyland era. This depressed state of affairs, plus the constant push by BL to improve productivity, led to horrendous problems with quality control, far worse than Jaguar had ever experienced before. Dealers were complaining about the amount of rectification work they had to carry out and owners were losing faith in the once prestigious marque.

More seriously, however, the same problems afflicted the whole of the BL group. A half-hearted attempt to improve quality came about with the announcement of the 'Quality 77' programme, which only really involved the use of posters and banners around the works, some pep-talks and a video. Jaguar's and BLs quality problems were by now too ingrained to be cleared up in this way. Morale was so low that inevitably the unions got involved and at a special meeting held by BL with the unions in March 1977 they gave assurances about the future of Jaguar. Plans were discussed about

bringing Jaguar production up to 1,200 cars a week within 10 years, with major capital investment, although there was little 'meat on the bone' about how this was going to be achieved.

On the plus side the original Jaguar apprenticeship scheme was still running and for a time Browns Lane became the centre of activity for *all* BL apprenticeship training, up to 600 at one time. Up to this time all apprenticeships had gone to young men, but for the first time in 1979 three Coventry girls took up engineering apprenticeships.

On 13 May 1978 Jaguar held its first Employees' Open Day at Browns Lane, but included the Radford plant and the service department at Kingfield Road. It was a real family day out, with access to the assembly lines, side shows, funfairs for the kids and

By this time the XJ6 had developed into the Series 2 models to meet changing legislation, particularly in the States. The model was well known for its quality problems. Here a car is being assessed for rectification in paint areas.

The first female engineering apprentices to join Jaguar in 1979 were, from left to right, Janet Goggins, Rebecca Yeowell and Pauline Gil.

a pipe band. Between 20,000 and 30,000 employees and families turned out. Later that year, courtesy of the employee services department, Jaguar's first range of merchandise went on sale, the forerunner to what is known today as the Jaguar Collection. Items such as Jaguar branded ties, t-shirts and scarves were available to buy, ideally timed for Christmas 1978.

With all this going on development was taking shape on the replacement, upgraded XJ saloon, the Series 3. The Series 2 XJs were even more successful than the Series 1 models had been, with over 127,000 being produced up to 1978 (against 98,500 Series 1s), despite poor build quality and continual minor warranty problems. However, without an entirely new product to take its place, the company looked outside of its own styling department for inspiration. Pininfarina of Italy were chosen and the result was the XJ Series 3 saloon introduced for 1979. Although looking very similar, the model was a significant improvement in design over the previous cars.

More changes for British Leyland were around the corner when, in November 1977, Michael Edwardes (chairman of Chloride Batteries) was appointed the new boss of BL. He recognised the flaws of the Ryder Report and set about implementing a recovery plan for British Leyland, which would again affect Jaguar at Browns Lane.

The car-making side of British Leyland was split into two divisions, one covering the quality end of the market and bringing together three prestigious Coventry marques to form a new company, Jaguar-Rover-Triumph Limited (JRT). This was under the control of another new man, William Thompson, who actually set up his office at Browns Lane. The new organisation had to be up and running within a couple of months, and one of the first proposals was to bring together the engineering departments of the three prestige marques, something director Bob Knight had previously fought against. He must have subsequently put up a good case, because not only did Jaguar remain separate, but he was also appointed the new managing director. Now at least Jaguar had one of their own at the helm, even if his power was diluted in real terms.

Things continued to go downhill, as quality had suffered further, partly because of BL management, partly because of poor morale at Browns Lane and partly because of finance. Even the parts suppliers had played their part in bringing about a decline in quality control at Jaguar, although sometimes unwittingly. BL controlled much of what was sourced, not least the purchasing of parts for existing and new models. Although there was still a purchasing department at Browns Lane, they had no real authority and their work had to be processed and approved by BL at the old Standard Triumph factory in Canley. BL based their purchasing on quantity and price, not quality, and Jaguar would suffer the indignities of this action. During 1978 60 percent of all warranty claims at Jaguar on new cars were attributed to faulty parts sourced from outside companies.

It was even becoming difficult to find good workers and managers in the Coventry area. The highly publicised problems at BL had led to a lack of trust, and who would want to work for a business in so much trouble? It did not help that during the splitting up of employees between Jaguar-Rover-Triumph and the other division (Austin-Morris), the latter had first bite of the cherry.

Jaguar and its people had fought constant battles to survive, and Jaguar-Rover-Triumph, plus the appointment of Thompson, helped just a little. The next battle, though minor, came with a new image for the JRT division. Despite frantic efforts by BL people to keep their spinning wheel logo and blue/white colours, to separate the division and at least give some sense of individualism to JRT, a lime green colour was chosen and started to appear around the factory and, of course, at the dealerships.

Sales of new Jaguars worldwide had dropped to the incredibly low figure of 14,861 cars by 1979 and a lot of this had been caused by the poor quality of the cars and components used in them. As mentioned earlier this was a uniform problem throughout BL but it hit Jaguar particularly hard as they were trying to sell prestigious expensive cars against ever-increasing competition from the likes of Mercedes and BMW.

To be fair to Jaguar's Coventry staff, a lot of problems came from other divisions within BL, such as the body-building and painting at Castle Bromwich, a constant source of so many problems during these years. The poor quality and design of some electrical components was another common source of complaint, but it was Coventry and the Jaguar name that suffered the criticism. Worse, Jaguar, like other factories within BL, had been directed to reduce costs, which meant that around 295 members of staff were lost through voluntary redundancy.

During the intense work to produce (and sell) more cars and rectify all the complaints against the 'new' XJ Series 3 saloons, the engineering department had already started work on a new Jaguar saloon and engine to replace the XJ Series models. They tried hard to preserve the 'Jaguarness' of such a vehicle, despite constant meetings, committee decisions and changes from the BL board. One of the better known aspects of this was that during the development of this new project (coded XJ40, mid-term changed to LC40 for Leyland cars but then changed back by Jaguar personnel!) Jaguar engineering staff deliberately designed the car not to accept a V8 engine because BL were considering dropping separate Jaguar engine production in favour of using the Rover V8 power unit. Such a move would not only have put the final nails in the coffin of Jaguar as far as the employees were concerned, but it would also have undoubtedly led to the eventual demise of sales in countries such as the US, because the Rover V8 was an original design from Buick and even the Americans had developed better engines since that one.

By 1979 industrial relations in the British motor industry were at their worst. All the BL companies were experiencing difficulties and lost production, not least Jaguar, where assembly workers went on strike over pay yet again in April. The dispute spread, resulting in all sorts of rumours, even giving rise to speculation that Browns Lane might close. Sir Michael Edwardes confirmed that Browns Lane workers would lose their jobs if they did not return to the shop floor. The tension resulted in one of the worst times for morale among employees at Browns Lane. They could gain little consolation from their colleagues at the other Jaguar plant in Radford, controlled at the time by another part of the BL company.

A glimmer of hope for Jaguar came about when Michael Edwardes announced more changes to the format of the car companies in September 1979. Realising problems with his original concept, Rover and Triumph would be moved over to join the Austin-Morris division as the volume end of the market and Jaguar (along with Land Rover) would be run separately at the luxury end. Another new company was set up, Jaguar Cars Holdings, into which Jaguar, Daimler, Browns Lane and Radford were all brought back under one banner. The cards had been shuffled yet again.

This was to be the last chance for Jaguar to succeed and prosper, back on its own feet, although still firmly part of BL. Sales had dropped to their lowest level in 20 years, production amounted to an abysmal 1.5 cars per employee and yet Jaguar still employed over 9,000 people. Profits had deteriorated to a loss of over £40 million for 1980. If the company could not be made to succeed this time round, there was absolutely no doubt that Jaguar in Coventry would disappear. So, another new man was sought to take over the reins at Browns Lane.

Enter Mr Jaguar

John Egan, born in Lancashire, could boast several connections to Jaguar and Sir William Lyons. Firstly he was a Lancastrian like Lyons, then he moved to Coventry with his parents when his father ran a garage in Foleshill Road (another connection, for this is where the original Swallow company had moved to in 1928). Egan was a student of Bablake School in Coventry and he became a very successful businessman. The connections with Jaguar continued as he set up the Unipart organisation for British Leyland, processing parts for all BL brands including Jaguar, and he also worked for Massey-Ferguson which provided other connections with the past through Standard.

He was offered the job of running JRT, but he turned it down, and it was only when Jaguar was separated that he became interested. In April 1980 he took up the position, at the age of only 40, of chief executive of the company and managing director of Jaguar Cars Holdings. A man with a strong passion for Jaguar and the Coventry area he showed immediate commitment to improving the business, its reputation and the lot of the workforce.

He took up his position over the weekend of 26 and 27 April when the factory was on strike. Michael Edwardes's plans that previous September had caused a storm, with the regrading of workers' pay in the hope of addressing differentials between skilled and unskilled workers. This had led to problems at Browns Lane, because even the ordinary assembly workers considered themselves more skilled putting a Jaguar together than someone down the road at Longbridge building a Mini. The strike at Jaguar spread to other companies within BL. Eventually the issues were cleared up throughout BL except at Jaguar, where workers remained on strike. Just four days before Egan joined the company, the *Coventry Evening Telegraph*

John Egan, a new man in Jaguar in 1980.

headlines read 'Nearly 3,000 Jag employees face the sack as the only part of BL workers still on strike.'

Egan immediately moved into Sir William Lyons's office at Browns Lane, where he spent the whole weekend negotiating with shop stewards and managers. After the discussions a vote was taken by a small majority a return to work was agreed. John Egan had little to offer at this stage but provided a personal commitment both to the job and the workers, and with this came a glimmer of light at the end of that very dark tunnel for everyone involved.

At Egan's first Jaguar board meeting, he heard via Mike Beasley of the possibility of Jaguar getting involved in a land exchange scheme with Coventry City Council, which would allow the Browns Lane site to be expanded at a cost of around £300,000. The extra space was urgently required if the company was to expand in the future, and this had previously been identified by Geoffrey Robinson, but the company was strapped for cash.

John Egan's prime task was to enthuse everyone involved in the company about quality control. His first target was the Castle Bromwich body and paint plant, and with

BL couldn't take everything away from Jaguar. The showroom area was being used as a miniature museum for some of the company's products. Here are an early Series 1 XJ6 (the actual car used by Sir William Lyons for many years), a 420G, a Mark 2, a Mark 1, a Mark V/Mark IV drophead coupé, an SS Jaguar 2.5-litre saloon (used by Lady Lyons), a Swallow sidecar, the very last E-type produced and an SS100 sports. Many of these cars are still in the hands of the JDHT today.

the help of Sir Michael Edwardes he was eventually able to take full control of this operation in 1980. This led to the building of a new computerised body storage facility at Browns Lane, still used today, into which the newly completed (and better quality) bodies from Castle Bromwich would be received, via modern purpose-built road trailers. Mike Beasley, another good Jaguar man, if a late arrival on the scene, was now plant director. Urged on by the enthusiasm of John Egan he promoted the new quality control programme throughout production.

At this time the company was still suffering major financial losses. In 1980 that loss amounted to some £47 million. But a sense of belonging had returned to Jaguar and the workforce and within 12 months Jaguar had taken back control of its sales and marketing areas with the appointment of new man Neil Johnson. Now operating out of Browns Lane again, although from temporary Portakabins close to the main office block, the move was on to create a new identity for Jaguar, but still based on the original concepts set by Lyons.

There was still a need to reduce staff, despite the fact that Jaguar achieved close to 80 percent of its budgeted production in 1980. A lot of people needed to go, although this was spread over a period of time. Initially 285 staff and 1,550 manual workers were lost. A total of 1,011 applications for redundancy were received.

The next step was to convince the dealers and particularly those in the US, who all came over to Browns Lane in 1981 to review the new model year's cars, now with a far more economical V12 engine, Jaguar was on the first rung of a tall ladder to climb back to success. The word 'quality' was on everyone's lips at Jaguar and this attitude was continued down the line to parts suppliers. John Egan instigated special test rigs to prove the longevity and suitability of parts for Jaguar motor cars, a system that had been in place years before at Rolls-Royce to ensure that every part was fit for the car.

Egan also set up a quality task force, which identified on average 1.8 faults per vehicle produced. Discussion groups of managers and their staff were established to highlight problems and to find solutions. Managers were encouraged to take cars home at night from the assembly lines, bring them back the following morning and report on their findings, identifying faults and methods of rectification. It was nothing really new – Lyons had done this himself back in the 1930s.

Along with all these changes in direction came a commitment to the workers to improve their lot over time even though workforce numbers generally had to be reduced. The problem was, however, that more engineers were required, and it proved exceptionally difficult to find the right people in Coventry at the time. Out of 35 such vacancies in 1980, only 19 could be filled. Cost savings were necessary in all areas and that even included restricting the number of phone calls made and the number of phones on site. A new slogan appeared to emphasise where the company was going – 'The Legend Grows' became the commonly seen caption on brochures, at dealerships and within the factory.

Eventually the Kingfield Road site was sold, allowing the removal of the engine reconditioning dept to the Radford factory and at the same time the service training school was relocated from Browns Lane to an upstairs floor in Radford, where it would eventually expand. Another favourable move was the return of the purchasing and cost control departments to Browns Lane from the old Standard factory in Canley.

Late in 1980 a proposed new pay offer to Jaguar staff was rejected, but as a measure of the enthusiasm of the workforce for the new regime, a vote of everyone at Browns Lane and Radford had resulted in a four to one vote against taking industrial action. By 1981 company losses had been reduced to £31 million and in 1983 Jaguar returned a profit for the first time in some years, although it was a modest figure of £9.6 million.

By 1982 Jaguar had turned the corner and John Egan announced a development programme called 'In Pursuit of Excellence – The Winning Team'. This was established to help everyone at Jaguar appreciate their role in the company. The first result of this was a series of video evenings for employees and family with refreshments and entertainment. Then followed a celebration of the 60th anniversary of the business by way of a second Open Day at Browns Lane on 14 August.

Meanwhile, the engineering department had finally completed work on Jaguar's third engine, the AJ6, a six-cylinder multi-valve unit which would eventually replace the XK engine still in production at the time.

The end result of all this change showed in dramatically improved quality, reputation and, of course, sales of Jaguars. For example, the XJ-S had gone through some lean times and there were lots of cars stacked up unsold. At one stage there was nearly a decision to drop the car completely. Egan saved the XJ-S, effectively re-launching it in 1981 with a revised engine specification to improve economy, the inclusion of some 'traditional' detailing with chrome and wood veneer and drastically improved build quality. The XJ-S became the first car to receive the new AJ6 engine in 1983, boosting the model range and sales further. The car went on to be the company's most successful sporting model of all time, remaining in production until 1996.

Then there were the existing XJ Series 3 saloons. With Egan's input, the setting up of a quality task force and a lot of work put in with parts suppliers, the models went through many changes and dramatic improvements and by the early eighties were selling better than ever. This led to the relaunch of the cars for the 1984 model year, giving greater emphasis to the Jaguar marque and moving the model name Sovereign over for their flagship model. The knock-on advantage of the improved sales of existing models was that Jaguar could take more time to get its all new model (XJ40) right. The launch of the new car was ultimately put back from 1983 to 1986.

1983 was an excellent year for Jaguar and for the remaining Coventry workforce which, by this time, was 35 percent smaller than when Egan joined the company, numbering just over 7,000 in total. Production now equated to 3.4 cars per employee, a record number for the company. Profits were back to realistic figures at £50 million. Record sales amounted to nearly 30,000 cars, of which half went to the valued North American market.

John Egan was given the accolade of Midlander of the Year, a fitting reward for his

By the 1980s limousine production had been moved to Browns Lane where bespoke DS420 motor cars were produced up to 1992.

hard work in bringing about Jaguar's revival. As some of the longer standing employees still say to this day, Egan gave everyone a hard time. He was a hard task-master but could sell his ideas well, which had a great effect on people and enabled him to achieve what he did.

In continued recognition of the hard work put in by employees Jaguar arranged a series of outings in 1983 commencing in April with special departmental competitions, then visits to see the XJ-S racing team in action at Donington and Silverstone, a bonfire night party and pantomime at Christmas. Also in 1983 the Jaguar Daimler Heritage Trust was formed to look after the company's archive, to develop interest in its heritage and to take back into Jaguar hands a number of important motor cars that had previously been with various owners and museums around the country.

Chapter Nine

A Sense of Belonging – 1984 to 1991

B Y THE mid-1980s Jaguar was so profitable it was already paying back money to BL, relinquishing its debt on the group. A lot of this profit, however, came from currency exchange rates rather than the cars, but at least the company was going in the right direction. The cars were selling well and the 'Legend had Grown'. Already there was talk about privatising the company or it being bought by another car company. Names like Ford, General Motors and even Toyota were associated with Jaguar for some time but nothing came of all this.

The Conservative Government was committed to privatisation and encouraged Jaguar to break away from BL. The then Trade and Industry Secretary Norman Tebbit announced that the profitable arms of BL, namely Jaguar and Unipart, would be sold off. This was the news that Egan had been waiting for and by mid-year the company was ready for the momentous move, already reporting profits of £40 million for the half year. Over the closing months of 1983 and early 1984 procedures were put in motion for the launch of a privatisation offer.

The final terms of the privatisation were agreed and in July 1984 the process began in earnest, not least with the appointment of

In February of 1984 the Browns Lane factory received another royal visit, this time from Prince Charles and Princess Diana, who were at the height of their popularity. This gave another lift to the workforce.

a new chairman of Jaguar, Hamish Orr-Ewing, more to satisfy the needs of the City than to actively play a part in the business. The share offer amounted to 177,880,000 ordinary shares of 25p each, which were offered for sale at the end of July.

Some were apprehensive about the whole aspect of privatising Jaguar, particularly BL, who would effectively lose out on future profits. As for the workforce, the opposite applied. Most of them had 'survived' through the bad days of BL and the virtual disintegration of Jaguar and all the company stood for, and all they wanted was to be cut free. Of course, they were driven on by the fact that they would also receive a small windfall with privatisation. Each employee was granted a stake in the new company of £400-worth of shares, on the proviso that they did not sell them for four years.

To combat fears of a rapid takeover of Jaguar by another company, the Government decided on taking what was loosely called a 'golden share' in the business, valid until

The London Stock Exchange on the morning dealing began in Jaguar shares.

December 1990. This effectively meant that the Government could block any attempts at a takeover until that time. On 6 August it was announced that no fewer than 320,000 applications had been received from investors, meaning that the share issue was over-subscribed some eight times. On the first day of trading the price of those Jaguar shares rose to a high of 181p. The flotation was a major success. BL made a lot of money from the deal and Jaguar became Jaguar once again.

John Egan, who was undoubtedly a good salesman in many ways, had actually achieved everything he had set out to do, and Jaguar was now back in charge of its own destiny. In his statement to the workforce in September Egan said:

> I would like to take this opportunity to thank my colleagues, the Jaguar employees, for their tremendous efforts and continuous support over the last few years which has enabled the company to stand on its own two feet.

It is very much due to their hard work that Jaguar has gained its independence and we can now look forward, together, to a successful future.

The benefits gained by our independence are enormous. For the first time in a decade we are now in the position to dedicate all of our company resources into the improvement of our Company and our product. We also have a stake in our own company.

The next move was for Jaguar to reassert itself in the parts field. In November they took control of their parts operation again, although it was still maintained and run on their behalf by Unipart from Baginton. Over 22,000 parts, all carrying the Jaguar name, were held by Unipart.

Jaguar's existing model, the Series 3 saloon, was still selling well in the 1980s despite the fact it was an old car by then and was still being produced on the old Triumph Mayflower line bought in the 1950s! Even in the 1980s Jaguar was behind the times, the wheels and tyres having to be manually lifted onto the hubs during assembly – a back-breaking job when you did it for a full shift.

The factory gates in Browns Lane after the return to Jaguar ownership – new gates and the use of the now common 'growler' motif. XJ6 saloons in the background await despatch.

The first annual general meeting of the new Jaguar Cars plc came about in 1985 when Sir William Lyons was still honorary president. At this point the company reported an expanded workforce of 10,000 employees, less industrial unrest than they had ever experienced, profits of £91.5 million and productivity of 3.6 cars per employee. To cap it all sales had increased yet again from the existing models, the XJ-S sports and XJ Series saloons.

The subject of expansion and congestion loomed again. The Browns Lane site now ran with 1,400 more people than it did in 1981, making it the largest single employer in the city. A public meeting was held at the Allesley Hotel just off Browns Lane on 24 January, at which the case for expansion and the need to ease congestion was made. Jaguar stressed that it was then putting around £1 million per day into the local economy and an answer was urgently required over expansion on the site. At the same time consideration had to be given to the increasing number of complaints from locals about the degree of traffic and even employee parking that was taking place in Browns Lane. At the same time moves were afoot to take on another site in Coventry for research and engineering development which would also relieve space at Browns Lane.

Within the Browns Lane site itself much work was afoot with building projects. For example, £1 million was being invested in a new laboratory complex near the GEC Block, £650,000 had been put into a new vehicle despatch compound at the back of the factory with service station-style fuelling facilities and extensive grounds on which

Celebrating a record 28,000 XJs produced in 1983 production workers pose for the camera with Wally Turner, then plant director at Browns Lane.

The picturesque village of Allesley as it is today. On the left is the Allesley Hotel, scene of many a heated word exchanged over the proposed expansion of the Browns Lane Plant in the 1980s.

to store cars awaiting despatch, and in the offices the heating system used wasted heat from the engine test facility next door.

A new wages building was built at a cost of £200,000. With privatisation came the need for more staff and the company expanded. Legal and treasury departments were now necessary to handle work previously carried out within the BL group. The expanded infrastructure also included new canteen facilities for the staff and the erection of a brand new Browns Lane social club on a sports field at the south gate entrance. It cost over £550,000 then and was expanded later to include a swimming pool and in 1989 a Fitness Factory (gym area). The social club is still on the same site today.

Finally there was to be a new face to Browns Lane in the form of a refurbished office complex with a conference centre and showroom. This involved some refurbishment

The Jaguar Sports and Social Club on Browns Lane, a vibrant facility for employees and associate members from within the Coventry community.

of the existing office suite. In the main it was felt that this should retain its original exterior style, but the old showroom (ex-ballroom) would be turned into a state-of-the-art theatre area for conferences and a new museum to house some of the company's collection of historic Jaguars and Daimlers. This was all completed in 1985 at a cost of £2 million, and remained in use until 2001 when the area was rebuilt again.

The proposed development at the back of the Browns Lane site affected an area of green belt land known as Coundon Wedge. This project actually dated back to the 1970s when

Jaguar had come a long way since the original office building was erected in the 1960s. A complete rebuild and refit took place in 1985, although the centre exterior core of the original offices was retained. Seen here on the right are the new reception area and new car showroom. Matching this building, to the left of the offices, were conference facilities.

Geoffrey Robinson had similar ideas in the British Leyland era, but at that time council planning was against it and there was little cash available to carry out the work. By the mid-1980s, Mike Beasley, currently managing director at Jaguar, was looking after the project, which was vital to the growth of the company if it was to stay in the Coventry

The new office complex with paved exterior and the revival of Jaguar signage, 1985.

area. Around 650 people attended the original meeting and there were many obstacles put forward by the Coundon Wedge Conservation Society. Indeed, they wanted Jaguar to build an underground tunnel through which to take the anticipated traffic – a far too costly proposal.

In preparation for what Jaguar felt was the inevitable, in order to make

more space available for employee parking and to ease congestion on site, a new perimeter road was made around the factory and a new car park built to the north. This was completed by the end of 1985. Extensive car parking facilities completed the scheme which is very much today as it was then in the 1980s.

The late Andrew Whyte, ex-Jaguar PR man and celebrated author, who in 1983 organised a get-together of ex-Jaguar apprentices and managers under the title 'Jaguar X'. The gathering was assembled from all over the world and included some well-known faces in the history of the company, including Lofty England, Bill Heynes and Wally Hassan, all seen here with John Egan, then chief executive of the company.

The workforce was by now more settled and was again expanding. Five hundred more jobs were created in 1985 in readiness for the launch of the new model, 320 of which were at Browns Lane. The Jaguar name, British racing green colour scheme and the famous 'leaper' re-appeared on the factory and on every bit of paperwork produced. Last, but by no means least, Jaguar had complete control over its manufacturing – for the first time ever it produced all its own bodies. The new empire encompassed Browns Lane for administration, trim and assembly, Radford for engines and transmissions and now the Castle Bromwich body plant in Birmingham for all fabrication and painting.

These were great times for the company, but the mood was dampened by the unfortunate death of the company's founder Sir William Lyons, who died at his home, Wappenbury Hall, on 8 February 1985. It was good that he was able to see the rebirth of the company and be involved in the development of the new XJ40 model that was to lead the company to further success. Lyons's wife, Greta, died at the age of 84 only 13 months later.

Each year, in September, a Long Service Dinner is held at Browns Lane. This one took place in the late 1980s within the new office complex, conference centre and museum facility. Employees were joined by their families and friends for the occasion.

Part of Egan's success with the workforce had been his approach to relationships. Early on he had implemented a 'hearts and minds' programme, bringing the workforces from all aspects of Jaguar production and development together. This meant using the in-house *Jaguar Topics* magazine to keep everyone informed of what was going on and the promotion of social events at which workers and their families could enjoy themselves and re-establish that Jaguar 'family' atmosphere. All of this led to better industrial relations, improved productivity and the ultimate aim of build and service quality.

Regarding the latter, quality control circles were set up to monitor progress, agree actions on problems and keep the move forward towards a significantly higher

Key personnel at Jaguar in the late 1980s were, from left to right: Wally Turner (Browns Lane plant director), Pat Audrain (purchasing director), Brian Savage (manufacturing, engineering director), Harry Fielding (quality control), Mike Beasley (manufacturing director), Gerry Lawter (Castle Bromwich plant director), Eynorn Thomas (engineering director), Jim Macaffer (production materials control) and Derek Waeland (XJ40 project manager).

standard within everything that Jaguar was involved with. This also affected training.

Jaguar's apprenticeship scheme, established after the war, like those of other manufacturers, involved on-the-job training specific to the company's needs and, in some cases, outside day release and/or evening courses. Egan took this a stage further, encouraging people within Jaguar to take up all manner of courses, some of which may not have been totally relevant to their particular job at that time. This covered a host of open learning courses covering anything from micro-computing to 'O' Levels, first aid to German. Middle and even higher managers were also encouraged to develop their skills, ultimately enhancing the company's assets.

Educationally Jaguar was also getting more involved with the local community. It sponsored a youth enterprise scheme with Coundon Court comprehensive school, where the sixth-form students had to set up and run a small business. Also, with the closure of some of the council children's homes, Jaguar got involved by adopting The Birches, a home for physically and mentally handicapped children.

The social side at Browns Lane was really coming into its own with more activity

The Queen Mother visiting Browns Lane, accompanied by (from left to right) Graham Whitehead, president of Jaguar North America; Ken Edwards, personnel director; John Edwards, financial director; Sir John Egan; -?- and Gavin Thompson, specialist car sales.

Prince Andrew, on a royal visit to Browns Lane, is here seen talking to an assembly worker preparing a V12 engine for installation.

than ever before in the history of the company. All the camaraderie at Jaguar had returned. The social club had no fewer than 8,000 employee members and associates.

As if to highlight the importance of Jaguar at this time a string of royal visits took place in the mid-1980s. As well as Prince Charles and Princess Diana, Prince Michael of Kent visited the factory. Prince Andrew came with the Queen Mother, and of course the Queen and Duke of Edinburgh returned yet again.

The overall quality of Jaguar cars had improved dramatically. This reduced the work in progress since fewer cars were awaiting rectification, and Egan set up new financial procedures to further advance company cash flow. Through agreement with suppliers payments were made later, nearly two months after delivery of products, while on the other hand payment was requested from dealers the moment that cars left the factory, in the UK at least.

On the factory floor the whole ethos changed. As well as attacking quality issues, there were stock matters to consider and for the first time the now commonplace aspects of 'just in time' stock management came into being at Browns Lane. Gone were the days when orders were placed with suppliers for a set number of components which were stored by Jaguar and lasted for a given length of production. From here on in, supply and storage of parts became the responsibility of the supplier, who would supply, sometimes on a daily basis, the stock needed for immediate use.

Jaguar resurrected an employee finance plan, enabling employees not only to buy cars but also to get access to personal loans for anything from £300 to £3,000.

Enter the Forty

Now Jaguar's attention could be focused on that new model, the XJ40. As 80 percent of all car sales had come from the XJ saloons, it was vital that the new car was right, to secure confidence in the privatised company. Egan and Jaguar had been given the extra time to perfect the car and they took good advantage of it. Over £500 million pounds was invested in the new car in terms of new plant, bringing in the latest technology to build and equip the vehicle, and by the time of its launch in 1986 five million miles of testing had been carried out. More work had been put into the XJ40 than any previous model. Styling had to retain elements of traditional Jaguars yet had to be modern, and it is perhaps fitting that even Sir William Lyons in his retirement took some hand in the car's final development. The body structure had to be significantly stronger but easier to build than the old XJ, and the XJ40 ended up being built from 25 percent fewer panels.

Similar emphasis was given to build. Traditionally engines had been dropped into the bodyshells from above the assembly line. This meant different angles at which the engines had to be poised and significant opportunity for

The latest technology was used in the XJ40, making it the most electronically advanced mass produced car in the world at the time. It subsequently went on to take the Top Car award from the Guild of Motoring Writers in 1986.

minor damage to components and bodies. These issues were addressed so that engines could be lifted up into the bodyshell on the new car.

The work was intense, but time was on Jaguar's side. When it came to the launch of the new car, it still retained the old name 'XJ6'. A special extended launch programme had been devised starting with a special presentation to the Institute of Mechanical Engineers in London early in 1986. Then in September the UK dealer launch took place at Browns Lane in a refurbished theatre complex developed out of the old showroom, coinciding with the press launch in Scotland.

A big plus for the workforce came during the summer shutdown in September when, after the dealer launches in Browns Lane, the 'circus' moved into a hall of the National Exhibition Centre in Birmingham for a period of four days. These were called 'J Days' and were for all employees and their families to see the car and to take advantage of Jaguar's hospitality as a thank you for the hard work put in by everybody.

Groups of 250 at a time were taken around the hall in a constant stream over the four days. As well as a speech from one of the company directors, the car was 'revealed' with an elaborate display of dry ice and fanfare and then everyone had the chance to view numerous displays, each one put on by a separate department with responsibility for the new car. This proved a great opportunity to cement relationships at Jaguar and to prove that John Egan's original commitment to his staff had been justified.

The launch razzamatazz did not stop there. After the J Days came a move of the circus to London for the City launch as a thank you to the big investors for their commitment to Jaguar. A film about the development and final launch of the car was also organised, an extensive production, which reached the UK TV screens on the very evening of the public launch of the car.

Actor George Cole (better known as Arthur Daley, the second-hand car dealer in the TV series) with an XJ40 among members of the service department.

The XJ40 was an instant success and Jaguar staff had worked hard to complete a virtual instant changeover from Series 3 to XJ40 production at Browns Lane. The intense workload included training on new plant and equipment and the removal of the remaining (low level) production of Series 3 V12s to another assembly line. Series 3 would remain in small-scale production until 1991 in the case of Jaguars and December 1992 in the case of Daimlers.

With production working flat out the principle was to boost numbers of cars leaving the factory by 100 percent. The car was designed from the start to be produced a lot quicker and in fact a target of 1,300 cars a week was set. This was not achievable

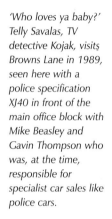

'Who loves ya baby?' Telly Savalas, TV detective Kojak, visits Browns Lane in 1989, seen here with a police specification XJ40 in front of the main office block with Mike Beasley and Gavin Thompson who was, at the time, responsible for specialist car sales like police cars.

because despite extensive training, everyone was working with new machinery on a new car and that affected production and thus sales dramatically.

As a mark of respect for the workforce Jaguar paid out a special Christmas bonus in 1986 of £600-worth of extra shares in the company to all employees. This one-off bonus was in recognition of twice hitting the company record, producing 1,000 cars a week. There was also a personal reward for John Egan, who was rightly recognised for his work in the motor industry when he was granted a knighthood in 1986, becoming Sir John Egan.

Some would say that Jaguar was back in the enviable position of not being able to produce enough cars to meet demand. In those early days, there was up to a 12-month waiting list for delivery of a new XJ40. This was, however, bad news for Jaguar, because it needed the higher production figures to meet that demand, otherwise people would go elsewhere, buying the competition and depriving the company of valuable income. Jaguar received the Queens Award for Technology Achievement in

1987 for the XJ40, another trophy for display alongside the Queen's Awards for Export Achievement of 1984, 1985 and 1986.

Production methods had been improved for the new model. The XJ40 was now easier and cheaper to build than any previous Jaguar model.

However, it was not all plaudits for Jaguar. The company, and John Egan in particular, came in for some criticism from Robert Aitken, Coventry's educational director, who claimed that John Egan had often been critical of the educational standards of schools and colleges, and that when Jaguar had previously run a youth training scheme it had refused to pay trainees an extra £7.50 a week on top of the £26.25 allowance from the Government. Aitken accused Jaguar of having little interest in Coventry and its local youngsters.

The truth of the matter was that Jaguar had regularly taken on substantial numbers of youngsters for engineering training. However, the company had been unable to get the full support of the allied unions for the scheme, which had thus had to finish in 1984. By this time Jaguar had managed to employ sufficient numbers of newly trained engineers

Sir John Egan receiving another award for Jaguar, the Queen's Award for Technology Achievement in 1987, from the Lord Lieutenant of Warwickshire.

The ever-expanding Browns Lane site had a new medical centre, opened in 1987, to cater for day-to-day industrial injuries but also with facilities for an optician and other specialists.

to fill its vacancies. By 1987 the situation had reversed, and on average 100 young people at a time were being recruited and trained, leading to no fewer than four types of apprenticeship: craft, technician, student sponsorship and graduate traineeship.

As a fitting celebration of the continued success at Jaguar, a third Open Day was arranged at Browns Lane on 3 May 1987. This time over 50,000 visitors came along.

Jaguar ran an employee opinion survey to evaluate what the workforce thought of the company, its products and procedures. From this a lot of useful information and suggestions came. One idea that the company adopted was a 'Speak Up!' scheme, enabling a member of the workforce to ask questions or come up with ideas and suggestions on a special form which only the co-ordinator for the project concerned would read. From this the information would be typed up and submitted to a company director for personal response which would then be forwarded back privately to the sender.

Another Coventry Site

Such was the success, both of the privatisation and the launch of the XJ40, that Jaguar took a major step forward in developing its engineering facility. Negotiations were

The Whitley site before Jaguar took it over. Much redevelopment work would take place before Jaguar would actually occupy it.

being carried out with Peugeot-Talbot over the old Chrysler engineering site at Whitley just off the A46. However, Coventry City Council were intending to develop this site as a high-tech business park, but they relinquished this in favour of Jaguar's proposal. At their council meeting on 14 May 1985 the leader of the council welcomed Jaguar's bid as a vote of confidence in the city.

John Egan negotiated the deal with an investment of over £37 million pounds and a plan to open in 1987. The site would employ around 600 people and enable the whole of the engineering and design facilities to be moved from Browns Lane, releasing valuable space for expansion there.

The building, of futuristic design, would be erected after the demolition of

The artist's impression of what Whitley would look like when Jaguar had refurbished the site.

Whitley from the air as it finally turned out under Jaguar ownership, one of the most advanced engineering facilities in the UK, expanded again in 2001 to incorporate a new styling studio.

500,000sq ft of existing works, plus refurbishment of other buildings and landscaping of the grounds. The very latest computerised technology with an energy efficient environment would enable the facility to be of world standing in the automotive industry and it was Egan's hope that, to offset the cost, other manufacturers would take advantage of Jaguar's facility. This was a bold consideration which never actually materialised as all manufacturers are naturally suspicious of each other when it comes to the development of new models and ideas.

Whitley did not open until May 1988, and a major recruitment drive took place to find the right calibre of people to work at the site, because these would be the future developers of Jaguar's new models. Within the first year of opening nearly 900 people were employed there. All engineering facilities were moved to Whitley from Browns Lane, leaving more space for production and administration.

While all this was going on things were not so good in financial terms. Late in 1987 the world crash of the stock markets cut Jaguar's US market share considerably. The British pound had strengthened further, reducing Jaguar's competitiveness overseas, and the British Government announced its worst ever balance of payments figures. Egan was able to switch from the intensive export of cars to the US, moving that demand to other countries, and for the first time since his arrival at Jaguar, less than 50 percent of cars were actually sold in the States.

Despite these trials and tribulations, by 1988 John Egan's weekly production figure of 1,300 XJ40s was eventually achieved. The production boom also applied to the evergreen XJ-S, then in its 13th year of production, which was speeding ahead in sales yet again. This was partly due to its success in the European Touring Car Championship in 1984, but more importantly was down to improved quality and yet another expansion in the model range with the launch of a proper two-seater convertible, ideally suited to the valued US market.

As if further proof was needed of John Egan's ongoing commitment to Jaguar, in February 1988 a joint venture was set up between Jaguar and GKN Sankey called Venture Pressings Limited. This £3 million investment at Telford in Shropshire finally took Jaguar completely out of the clutches of the old BL companies as the business was set up to press and supply body panels to Castle Bromwich for the assembly of car bodies.

Another new development was the building of a computerised body store at Browns Lane to handle the finished bodies from Castle Bromwich awaiting build. The

The extensive body store opened at Browns Lane in 1988.

project was completed in 1988 and accepts bodies brought in from Castle Bromwich by the company's own transport, stores them and then delivers them automatically via conveyor to the assembly lines as required, to specific order.

Not content with the launch of the XJ-S convertible, Jaguar looked to improve its market share with a younger audience. Jaguar had long been considered a builder of old man's cars, ideal for company directors and chairmen but not for the ever-expanding group of young executives and high flyers. So, in May 1988, Jaguar set up another joint venture, this time with the TWR Group (which had led Jaguar to success in the European Touring Car Championship with XJ-Ss) to form JaguarSport Limited. Based in Kidlington near Oxford the new company would supply modified versions of the Jaguar car range in small-scale production.

Initially XJ-Ss and then XJ saloons were built at Browns Lane in the normal way but then shipped down to Kidlington where they were given the 'sport' treatment. Bespoke paint finishes, fatter alloy wheels and tyres, colour co-ordinated body kits, upgraded interiors and in some cases modifications to engine, suspension and brakes were added.

Jaguar's racing pedigree had always been of immense importance, initially in the 1950s at Le Mans, then in strengthening the market for the XJ-S with the European Touring Car Championship in the early 1980s. There had also been limited success in the States with the Group 44 racing team initially promoting the E-type, then the XJ-S and later a specially built sports racing car. John Egan looked to this area for another marketing enhancement and the thought of competing at Le Mans was resurrected, eventually leading to success in 1988 and 1990, giving a well deserved boost to worldwide car sales.

After the Le Mans win in 1988, at the motor show Jaguar showed a one-off prototype supercar, the XJ220 as it was called. Effectively hand-built on the basis of the Le Mans racing car, this was a private project carried out at Whitley by Jaguar engineers led by their boss, Jim Randle. A massive mid-engined V12 500bhp car, the response was so good that Egan decided it had to go into small-scale production, although later the design would be significantly modified and finally built at a special new TWR JaguarSport facility in Bloxham, Oxfordshire, now the home of Aston Martin DB7 production.

Returning to general production and the economic climate, despite everything Jaguar produced more cars in 1988 than they had ever done before in the life of the company – a total of 52,000 cars. Some of this success was down to Egan's offensive

After the Le Mans success in the 1950s that helped Jaguar's prestige, the company returned successfully in 1988 and 1990. Here the three winning cars in the 1988 race parade past the chequered flag line astern to rapturous applause from all the Jaguar fans.

on other markets like Germany, and the fact that Jaguar had been setting up its own distribution companies in places like Japan. However, the strategy at Browns Lane was changing from increased numbers of cars to reduced costs. A detailed study of every aspect of the business from investment in new machinery to the canteen was carried out. The company needed to find £120 million in order to maintain its profitability in the light of anticipated lower car sales.

During this time the XJ40 went through various development stages, rectifying some of the problems, particularly with bodywork and electronics, that were associated with the earlier cars. By 1990 quality had substantially improved, the 3.6-litre engine had been increased in size to four litres and sales were still going well, but cash was in very short supply. Jaguar was still not generating enough cash to develop new models or even to continue in its present vein. After all the hard work put in by John Egan and the workforce, the company just was not viable. Money was required urgently and Jaguar had to find a new owner or partner.

Chapter Ten

Hands Across the Sea: Ford Involvement 1990 – present day

EGAN looked elsewhere for assistance in keeping Jaguar afloat. He chose to negotiate with the American General Motors Group in the hope of them taking a minority stake in the business, leaving Jaguar independent. This was early in 1989 but later in the year the Ford Motor Company announced that it had purchased a 15 percent stock-holding in Jaguar. Jaguar, of course, was still protected by the Government's 'golden share' in the business, which meant that a hostile takeover was not possible. However, that protection was due to end in December 1990, but as it turned out the Government changed its mind and relinquished its hold on the company almost immediately.

This left the way clear for Ford to make an offer to buy Jaguar outright, which it did on 2 November, offering a price substantially above what even General Motors would have offered. By this time Ford held 77 percent of the shares and in essence the deal was done. The shareholders also had their final say and over 99 percent of votes went in favour of the Ford bid. The offer of £8.50 per share was exceptional and the deal was struck at a cost of £1.6 billion.

The Ford Motor Company was at the time the second-largest producer of motor vehicles in the world and had a very well established UK arm based in Dagenham in Essex and Halewood in Liverpool. It was also used to takeovers and in the US owned Lincoln, perhaps Jaguar's closest rival in that country within the Ford empire.

Although the Jaguar workforce had had no involvement in, or prior knowledge of, the previous company changes (with BMC and later Leyland), this time they had good warning. When it all finally happened John Egan's letter to the workforce at the time laid out the truth and promises for the future:

> ...I view Ford's ownership of Jaguar with a great deal of confidence and excitement. Several assurances have been given by Ford regarding our future;

Sir John Egan with Lindsey Halstead of Ford, making the formal announcement of the Ford bid.

our headquarters will remain in Coventry and manufacturing will continue in the West Midlands. Whitley will be maintained as our Engineering Centre and there will be continuity of employment, pension rights and the level of employee benefits. Ford intends that we will have a high degree of operating independence with the Jaguar management and employees continuing to be responsible for day to day operation. Ford recognise, and will use our strengths positively.

At the time of the Ford takeover Jaguar's sales were running at about 5 percent down on the previous year. The revised business plan for 1990 allowed for a production figure of 53,000 cars. The company had already launched its 1990 model range which, although based on the same cars as previously, incorporated many new features, not least the adoption of a 4-litre version of the AJ6 engine.

The workforce had mixed feelings about the takeover. Some thought it was the end of Jaguar as they knew it and considered Ford a downmarket company producing cars like the Ford Escort. Others, some long-termers, were just 'dulled' by it all, after the previous changes, but the majority, although a little apprehensive, thought little about whether it would have a major effect on them or not. In fact most knew that Jaguar was in real trouble and might not survive without help from Ford.

During those early months with Ford, a joint Ford/Jaguar transition team was set up to review the company's strengths and weaknesses, and from their findings suggestions were put forward to the new Jaguar board about changes. That new board incorporated two Ford nominated directors, Lindsey Halstead, chairman of Ford Europe, who held a non-executive role with Jaguar, and John Grant, who became deputy chairman of Jaguar. It was also inevitable that Sir John Egan would finally leave the company. This he did in March 1990, and his place was taken by a Ford man, William Hayden CBE, who had been the vice-president of Ford in Europe. On the takeover he became a member of the transition team.

Bill Hayden, the new Ford boss for Jaguar, with Sir John Egan during the transition period.

The change process was slow and co-ordinated, unlike the British Leyland days, and the very first change that really didn't have anything to do with Ford, affected all staff at Browns Lane and other Jaguar plants. Compass Catering took over all the catering arrangements. Vending machine areas were renamed 'Pitstops' and they introduced a healthy eating programme throughout their sites. A new double-decker restaurant opened offering a carvery upstairs and a traditional restaurant with take-away service on the ground floor. There was also a Jaguar Grille restaurant, a visitors' dining room and a large function room. Another change decided by Jaguar and operational from the start of 1990 was the 'Health and Heart' programme, with the on-site medical centre offering advice and health checks to all staff.

The major task ahead of Ford however was just to ensure the survival of Jaguar as a company. Completely strapped for cash prior to the takeover, a massive influx of capital was required to move it forward. Hayden's inaugural announcement to all staff in June centred on just two important points. One, that he was confident Jaguar could overcome its current problems and prosper, and second, if it was to achieve its potential, everyone had to contribute to improvements and be prepared to accept change. Such comments were not so very different to those made by John Egan or William Lyons!

During this period the issue of the Browns Lane 'relief road' at the back of the factory had been settled and work had started. The route of the new road crossed Coundon Wedge, although Coventry City Council issued strict controls to minimise damage to the environment and surrounding countryside with landscaping and mature trees to be planted to screen the road from surrounding properties and to ensure the new road blended in with the countryside.

The road commenced from the roundabout of Birmingham Road and Holyhead Road and took a reasonably straight course around the back of the factory to a new roundabout from which it would meet up with Long Lane. At the roundabout a left turn would bring all traffic to a brand new Jaguar main gate entrance near the newly built north car park. The whole project cost around £4 million, of which Jaguar paid £2 million. It relieved 95 percent of company traffic from Browns Lane, completely removed the obstruction of employees cars parked at the kerbside and satisfied the local community.

Two further plus points at the time came when in June of 1990 a World Jaguar Weekend was organised to celebrate Jaguar's 40-year association with the Le Mans 24-Hours race in France. A civic reception was held at the Coventry Museum of Road Transport where there was an exhibition of Jaguar art. The whole weekend over 9 and 10 June included an International Jaguar day at Charlecote Park near Stratford, a gala dinner and a Jaguar race day at the Donington circuit near Derby. The second point was that Jaguar won the Le Mans race for the seventh time.

The Coundon Wedge Drive project was finally opened in 1991 by the Lord Mayor of Coventry and Mike Beasley on behalf of Jaguar.

Meantime Mr Hayden and his Ford team were making in-roads into Jaguar's problems. Specific Ford quality measures were brought in and these included a total revision of house-keeping within the Browns Lane plant. He, over a period of time, was able to release Jaguar and its employees from the myriad restrictive practices that had dominated the industry for many years.

As a boss, Hayden was respected rather than liked; he was a very hard taskmaster who told it as it was. Some would eventually call him the 'hatchet man', but he had a job to do in bringing Jaguar into the modern world of automotive production. Quality, bringing down costs and improving sales were his priorities – again not so different to how Lyons viewed things back in the thirties.

Sales fell again in 1991 and the financial results revealed a £66 million loss, which led to the old problem of lay-offs followed by voluntary redundancies and then enforced redundancies, resulting in a 30 percent drop in the total workforce within a few months. Those employees still around at Jaguar not only benefited from Ford's cash injection into the business and the security that came with it, but several Ford procedures and benefits were implemented, not least the Privilege Ford Purchase Scheme, allowing employees to purchase Ford motor cars on special plans, a system that, with a few changes, still applies today.

The social side at Browns Lane continued, albeit with fewer people. One of the highlights of the year was the opening of a new cancer ward at the Walsgrave Hospital, furnished by donations from employees of Jaguar. At Browns Lane itself the Jaguar Daimler Heritage Trust took control of the company's archive and they got a curator to look after the vehicles.

The first major model change took place in 1991, a complete facelift for the XJ-S model, from then on known as the XJS. Over £50 million was invested in the new car, which involved entirely new presswork, interior and a car of enhanced quality. To counter this, Hayden stopped all work on the supposed replacement for the XJS, coded XJ41.

On the saloon car front, quality was improving. There was a new 3.2-litre engine for the cheaper models and in the annual *What Car?* Awards, Jaguar was runner-up, pushing competitors BMW and Mercedes out of the top ranking.

The styling department at Whitley. In the foreground is a mock-up of what would have been the Jaguar F-type sports car, a project developed during Sir John Egan's period but cancelled by Ford as unsuitable for production. The men include Keith Helfet, styling manager, David Boole, Jaguar PR, John Egan, Chris Columbo and the then Minister for Transport.

By 1991 the Jaguar workforce had been reduced from 12,000 to 8,000, and the most painful part of the Ford business plan was perhaps over. Quality had been dramatically improved with complaints averaging just 20 percent of what they had been when Ford took over the company. Productivity was up by more than 20 percent. Assembly practices had also been improved. Part of this process of improvement was the introduction of what Ford called JQ1 – a special Ford award issued to a plant when it achieved an above average level of excellence. Jaguar's Radford plant achieved this

award in 1991. Browns Lane was still working towards it.

The worst aspects of the Ford takeover appeared to be over, and despite a continued world recession in quality car sales, Jaguar was looking to the future, by this time confident that it would remain independent and individual from the massive Ford empire and the other products it produced.

Sally Gunnell, Olympic sports star, raising money for the BBC Pudsey Bear appeal 'Children in Need' at Browns Lane in the 1990s.

Change at the Top

Bill Hayden had done his job and duly retired from the company and Ford in March 1992, to be replaced by a new man, Nick Scheele. Another Ford man of 26 years, he had most recently run the purchasing operation for their North American assembly plants and their Mexican plant. He had always been earmarked for the Jaguar chairman's job.

Nick Scheele was much more personable than Hayden but nevertheless still had a hard job ahead. He now had the opportunity to stamp his success on the company and the workforce instantly took to him. In his opening message to everyone he commented:

> Since my arrival at the beginning of the year the single, overriding impression I have of Jaguar is the total dedication and loyalty of you, the employees. This is particularly surprising considering the difficult and gloomy period that you have faced over the last eighteen months. My commitment to you is that I will do everything in my power to ensure that loyalty is rewarded with a bright and secure future for the Company.

Good words from a good man and he kept his word.

Coinciding with this statement the once prototype XJ220 supercar went into a limited production run of 350 cars, although not in Coventry. The cars were built at a small new factory as part of the JaguarSport operation, a joint venture between Jaguar and TWR Racing. The first 10 of these super sports car were planned for delivery later in 1992.

Scheele had more important issues to deal with because although sales had marginally improved into 1992, they were still less than 22,500, under half what the company was producing at its peak in the late 1980s. More lost their jobs but Ford allowed the important investment in new models to continue, although these would have to be derived from the existing cars, the XJ40 and XJS. Over £60 million would go into the next saloon model with more to come on the sports car and even more on a new Browns Lane assembly line.

During this period Jaguar set up an employee development programme, enabling everyone to increase their skills to maximise their potential at work. The scheme was well accepted by everyone and all manner of courses were introduced, including specialist knowledge, national certificates and even the Open University.

The first thing, however was the final demise of the XJ Series 3 saloons. The XK six-cylinder engined model was deleted just after the XJ40 was announced. The V12 engined versions remained in production however, the last Jaguar leaving the line in 1991 and the very last Daimler model in November of 1992, seen off by Nick Scheele himself. His wife used the penultimate car for some time!

Coinciding with this demise came the last of the Daimler DS420 limousines to leave the limousine shop, which subsequently became known as special vehicle operations.

Then in March 1993, as well as improved quality for the existing saloons to include driver's air bags, Jaguar announced the V12 and Daimler equivalents, an engine, although based on the original version, now of six litres capacity, more economical and brought up to date.

Jaguar's Radford site had excellent training facilities, not least in computers, and the facilities were made available to the local TEC (Training Enterprise Council) and were

The very last XJ Series 3 saloon, which left the line in 1992 with a quiet celebration.

used for ex-employees and local unemployed people to gain training in this up and coming area.

It was during the summer holidays of 1993 that everyone was to see the most major change at Jaguar effected by Ford – a stunning £86 million upgrade in the assembly line which would form part of a major five-year pro-gramme. As mentioned earlier Jaguar's production line had been installed in the mid-1950s, purchased second-hand from another car producer. Now this was totally ripped out and replaced with the latest state-of-the-art assembly track system.

The new system was made up of a one kilometre long assembly track with overhead mounted cradles that accepted the car bodies from the body store and moved them along to where they met up with the engine and transmission assemblies. A 'doors off' assembly system was employed where the doors were built up separately and returned to the bodyshell later in production. The whole system allowed more space between lines, a much cleaner working environment, was less stressful to the workforce and permitted the use of 'just in time' stock management at the trackside. It took a mere four weeks to install and provided no problems when first initiated. Under the old assembly line system a maximum of 16 cars an hour could be assembled. Now with the overhead facility this was up to 25. Browns Lane was now not only up to date, but ahead of some of the competition.

This was one good step forward, but Jaguar would have to make others. The new 1990 Act relating to issues of environmental protection would affect all car manufacturers. A lot of money would and still needs to be invested in making cars more environmentally friendly and economical.

The next change at Browns Lane affected the sawmill area, where the wood for the famed Jaguar interior veneers arrives and is processed. The installation of three new spraybooths, the first in use in the UK, made for a more efficient and environmentally friendly department.

As an addition to the model range to enhance sales Jaguar also introduced their Insignia Scheme, utilising the special vehicle operations department at Browns Lane. With the aid of the very experienced trim staff who used to work on the limousines, Insignia allowed for the design and fitment of bespoke trim and finishes to XJ40 and XJS models. Very much a one-off service at substantial extra cost, it had limited success until 1994 and although the scheme is no longer listed today, Jaguar will still do anything you wish to a Jaguar, providing you have the money!

Since the early 1990s Jaguar has been an equal opportunities employer, and has a joint equal opportunity sub-committee to look into and uphold such procedures. They ensure that everyone within Jaguar lives up to the high standards set by the company, something that is a tribute to Jaguar and Coventry.

On the quality side another commitment was made by everyone in order to achieve British Standard BS5750. Over the course of September to November all three Jaguar plants were subjected to assessment and achieved the award, another step on that important road to total quality control.

1993 sales had taken a turn for the better. Standing at nearly 27,500 they were over 20 percent up on the previous year. Jaguar won another luxury car award for the XJ40 and yet more enhanced models made their debut.

For 1994 another face-lifted XJS came on stream with all enveloping bumper bars, a brand new AJ16 version of the six-cylinder engine, more enhancements and better standards of equipment. For the XJ40, a new S (sport) model was introduced in an effort to encourage a younger market for saloons and this was soon followed by another 'final fling' for the Forty, when the Gold version was introduced offering a high degree of standard specification for a low price. Despite the knowledge that the XJ40 was actually running out later on in 1994, it was still finding new homes and achieved, for the second year running, the *What Car?* Award for best luxury car.

Nick Scheele was involved in the NSPCC charity and in May 1994 arranged the first of several gala dinners at Jaguar to raise money for the cause. This started a year of fund raising for the NSPCC, resulting in a total of £400,000 being raised.

In June 1994 the Browns Lane plant and the Castle Bromwich plant were rewarded with the prestigious Ford Q1 award. The presentation for Browns Lane was received

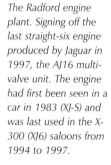

The Radford engine plant. Signing off the last straight-six engine produced by Jaguar in 1997, the AJ16 multi-valve unit. The engine had first been seen in a car in 1983 (XJ-S) and was last used in the X-300 (XJ6) saloons from 1994 to 1997.

by the then plant director Richard Hudson. It had taken three years to achieve this goal of 'continuing to meet and exceed customer expectations'.

Towards the end of 1994 the association between Jaguar and Venture Pressings Limited was terminated as Ford's Halewood plant in Liverpool took on the supply of body panels for Jaguar cars.

A New Dimension

Things had been going well for Jaguar under Nick Scheele. The workforce was respected and happy, the cars were built to a much better quality and Jaguar was still well regarded in the Coventry community. The need for new models was, however, pressing and working hard in the background the Whitley engineering staff were bringing to fruition the first new cars under Ford ownership. Coded X-100 and X-300, both would be based on the older models but were to prove a significant move ahead for the company and therefore a tribute to everyone's hard work.

The Jaguar employees were to be the first to witness the success of the finished product in the new saloon (X-300) aptly named, yet again, XJ6. To celebrate the finish of the project and as a thank you, Nick Scheele arranged another Open Day at Browns Lane, which an estimated 15,000 employees and their families attended. The assembly line was laid open to view, there were lots of side shows to interest everyone, including the kids, and there on display in a specially erected marquee in front of the office block was the new car in all its splendour – the 'New Series XJ6'.

As for the car, it was a much improved saloon to the best quality ever produced by Jaguar up to that time. Although based on the previous XJ40 floorplan, all the outer panels were new, it used the latest version of the six and 12-cylinder engines, it was easier to build and longer lasting. Over the course of the next few months the car would achieve many accolades, not least *What Car?* Luxury Car of the Year and the most Beautiful Saloon Car in the World – Jaguar had achieved what Ford had requested.

The Whitley engineering site also achieved accreditation, winning its ISO 9001 quality assured certificate. Finally, there was yet another royal visit, this time by the Queen, to the Browns Lane plant.

So by 1995 Jaguar was in fine condition. The Jaguar name was now 60 years of age and to commemorate this the XJS entered its final year of production as the celebration model. Unfortunately one downside to this year would be the death of 'Lofty' England, one-time right-hand

Another royal visit to Browns Lane, this time by the Queen and Duke of Edinburgh. On the left is Pat Smart (then responsible for the royal cars), while Nick Scheele is on the right.

man to Sir William Lyons, the man behind the competition successes on the track in the 1950s and managing director himself before he retired.

Success followed with the cars in 1995. In the first nine months of sales 30,523 cars were sold, 42 percent up on the previous year and more than all the cars sold in 1994. Long wheelbase versions of the X-300 saloons became available, enhancing the range, and there was already commitment from the Board of Trade to support the modernisation of the Castle Bromwich factory to produce a new smaller saloon coded X-200.

Another new initiative, fully supported by Nick Scheele, was the 'Customer Relationship', a procedure to ensure the utmost customer care, elements of which still exist today to ensure that Jaguar buyers get the best from their cars.

For 1996 Jaguar announced a limited run of 200 Daimler models to commemorate the 100th anniversary of the Daimler company, Coventry's oldest surviving car name. By contrast in May the company announced the withdrawal of the XJS from the company car range in readiness for an entirely new sports car, the XK8, first seen at the Geneva Motor Show in March but launched in the UK at our own motor show in October.

The second new car from Ford money, the XK8, although using the old XJS floorplan, was otherwise all new. It boasted the very latest technology, including a new Jaguar V8 engine, produced at the Ford Bridgend plant in Wales rather than at Radford, which had carried an investment of £200 million. With this came the demise of both the V12 and six-cylinder engines, leaving Radford to produce axle assemblies for all Jaguar models. The car was so successful that a record 1,825 cars were sold in the first month.

Coinciding with the launch of the XK8 came another Browns Lane open day. Jaguar also won another top award, the Britain's Top Manufacturer Achievement Award from the *Engineer* publication and the Browns Lane social club received the 'Clubland Oscar' award for 1996, when it was voted the best company based social club in the UK.

In 1996 David Boole, Jaguar's PR director, died suddenly. He was a strong supporter of local Coventry matters and indeed helped raise over £400,000 for a new centre for abused children. When the centre was opened in Whitefriars Street by Princess Margaret, it was renamed Boole House.

The company celebrated 75 years in 1997. On 6 June the whole frontage of the Browns Lane plant was turned over to a massive celebrity ball, hosted by Nick Scheele, which raised £50,000 for the NSPCC Kids In Coventry Appeal. Sports, TV, film and entertainment celebrities came along and after dinner an auction was held that raised a further £20,000 for the charity.

Another opportunity arose for Jaguar to celebrate and raise money for charity, this time BEN, the motor industry's own charity, at their residential home at Town Thorns. Over the weekend of 16 and 17 August the grounds of the home were dominated by Jaguar displays from the early days of Swallow through to the latest models and superb displays of art and memorabilia.

As far as the cars were concerned, by April the last V12 engine had left the line and the run-down of XJ6 production was taking place in readiness for the next generation of Jaguar saloon, coded X-308. The new cars, all still based on the old model but with trim improvements, enhanced suspension and not least the adoption of the V8 engines, now in two engine sizes, came about in September of 1997. The transition to V8 engines was now complete.

Also in 1997 a major announcement took place concerning the Jaguar Daimler Heritage Trust. It was to build a new £1 million museum and visitors centre on the Browns Lane site. This opened in 1998 and included the resiting of the company's public affairs department to the upper floor.

Things were moving quicker than ever for Jaguar in 1998. Since Ford had taken over

Just a small selection of the historic vehicles owned and preserved by the Jaguar Daimler Heritage Trust, seen here in their Heritage Centre built on the Browns Lane site.

the Browns Lane plant had been significantly redeveloped. Castle Bromwich was under major development to make the new S-type medium-sized saloon, and in February it was announced that Jaguar would be be taking control of the ex-Ford Halewood plant in Liverpool to build another entirely new car, the X-type. Whitley was also undergoing major reconstruction to meet the demands of all the work required for what would be a four-model line up, and also managed to achieve Ford's Q1 status.

There was also the launch of the first supercharged sports car, the XKR sports, and the public announcement of the XK180 car concept. Jaguar also declared its participation in the Government's New Deal programme for unemployed youngsters, which would give them the opportunity to learn, get advice and eventually find full time employment. The company also received a Community Citizenship award from Coventry City Council in recognition of its work eliminating discrimination and fostering equality in the workplace.

Another major success story was the announcement that after several years hard work the company had achieved formal recognition for ISO 14001, the international standard on environmental issues. Finally, in 1998 the company achieved record sales. More cars were sold than ever before in the company's history.

The following year, 1999, was similarly important for Jaguar. Morale in the workplace had never been better, standards were at their highest and the S-type was finally launched, produced separately at the Castle Bromwich plant in Birmingham.

The sad news was that after seven years Nick Scheele resigned from his position as chairman of Jaguar Cars, leaving to rejoin Ford, initially in Europe and then the US. He had done a splendid job with Jaguar and he has been much missed by everyone within the company.

The new man at the helm was Wolfgang Reitzle. This ex-BMW director was also in charge of Ford's new Premier Automotive Group, which brought together Jaguar and other Ford premium brands Aston Martin, Volvo and Lincoln, later to be joined by Land Rover when Ford took control of that company from BMW. A new position was also created of executive director at Jaguar, which was filled by the then manufacturing director Mike Beasley. A new man, Jonathan Browning, was appointed managing director.

Sales of cars worldwide amounted to another record of 75,312 cars in 1999 and at the end of the year Jaguar invited all employees, friends and guests to a Millennium Celebration at the NEC in Birmingham. Taking over a complete hall at the centre there were displays of new and historic Jaguars and Daimlers depicting every year from 1922. There were also major displays from the various departments within the company, suppliers and the clubs.

At the beginning of the new millennium one of the first changes to be made by Browning and Beasley was the instigation of the '6 Sigma' process to improve quality throughout all operations. Still committed to training, Jaguar also retained an Investors in People Award given by the Coventry and Warwickshire Chamber of Commerce. Jaguar's commitment to the local Coventry community was also strengthened in 2000

by the setting up of 'Jaguar in the Community' and the building of Jaguar Education Business Partnership Centres at Browns Lane and Castle Bromwich, a joint exercise with Coventry and Birmingham educational services.

Facilities are provided on the Browns Lane site for training, audio-visual displays, talks and use of computer technology. Local schools can make use of these facilities, bringing along children from 4 to 18 years of age to learn and appreciate the relevance of such training to the employment world. Jaguar sponsor the centre, and also supply a couple of minibuses for schools' use.

Jaguar continues to attract accolades. The company has received the Queen's Award for Enterprise in International Trade in recognition of its export achievements over the years, and Browns Lane specifically has received the Gold Award from JD Power, a US-based organisation, confirming the continued improvement in quality of the XK and XJ models.

By 2001 the Radford Sports and Social Club had received an £800,000 refurbishment, although by this time the actual ex-Daimler works had gone through a planned closure with the demise of all Coventry-built engines. Axles and other components are now assembled at Browns Lane.

Another change at the top saw Jonathan Browning resign in favour of Mike Beasley who became and is the

The Business Partnership scheme between Jaguar and the local educational community – a new building within the Browns Lane Plant complex.

All that now remains of the Radford factory, the fire station.

The rebuilt (for the second time) office and administration block at the Browns Lane plant with reception on the left, the original centre section and the contemporary coffee shop to the right.

A special statue was commissioned of Sir William Lyons which now overlooks the new building. To its side the Jaguar Daimler Heritage Centre ensures the continued safe-keeping of the company's history.

current managing director of Jaguar Cars Limited. The Browns Lane headquarters of Jaguar received another facelift during 2001 when the office block was completely refurbished with new external design (although retaining the 1953 façade of the centre

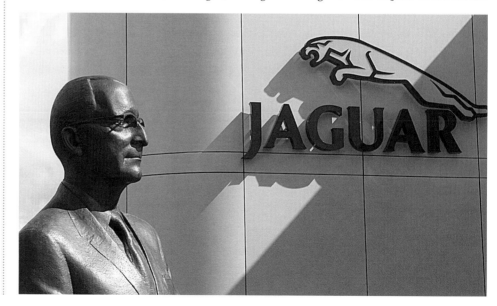

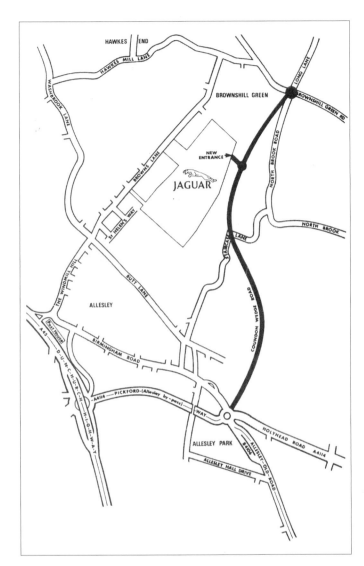

section), a new reception area, a gallery walk-through area with inter-active displays, a lecture theatre with the very latest audio-visual technology and even a contemporary coffee lounge.

Jaguar has come a long way since its humble beginnings in Blackpool in 1922. From 1928 and the move to Coventry, it is difficult to imagine that even William Lyons himself could have foreseen the progress the company has made in that time. Despite many ups and downs Jaguar has come through stronger than ever. It employs Coventry people, brings prestige to the city and is known the world over as a producer of fine motor cars.

Jaguar now boasts four model ranges, the X-type made in Liverpool and the S-type made in Castle Bromwich, with engines for all cars produced in Bridgend in Wales. Browns Lane, however, is still the home of Jaguar and its head office. It continues to produce the top of the range models, XJ and XK.

Jaguar's Browns Lane plant celebrated its 50th anniversary in September 2002, a fitting reminder that the legend of Jaguar lives on.

Browns Lane Factory Tour – Today

MANY operations are no longer carried out at Browns Lane. Body painting is done at Castle Bromwich, seating is made up under contract by Lear in Walsgrave, as are dashboards, and engines are assembled in Bridgend. The whole Browns Lane plant now operates on a staff level of about 2,000, including administrative posts, yet they produce more cars and to a higher standard than in the 1950s.

The impressive front gates and entrance to the Browns Lane plant, although the giant radiator grille has been removed. All traffic enters and exits from here to avoid using Browns Lane.

Bodies are transported from Jaguar's Castle Bromwich factory to the body store in the company's own covered lorries.

Once a body is selected it moves automatically by conveyor to the assembly hall where it mounts on to a cradle for the majority of its journey on the line.

The assembly line today in the same building as the 1950s. Compare this photograph with that on page 104, taken from the same point in the 1960s. At that time up to 10 cars an hour could be turned out, but now it is 25.

The body gains various components and trim along the line. Here the dashboard is a complete assembly, built up by an outside company and supplied to the line as one complete unit, hydraulically assisted into position.

The V8 engines are assembled in Wales but still require some work at Browns Lane, including the mating of gearboxes before joining the body.

Front and rear axle
assemblies are made
up at Browns Lane on
a different line but
within the main
assembly hall.

In the 1960s carpet
trim was made up of
individual pieces,
either glued or clipped
in position. These days
carpets are supplied
pre-formed in one
complete unit for ease
of fitment.

Although the Jaguar leather seats are made up by a contract company, the leather itself is still cut and inspected at Browns Lane by experts who look for any imperfections.

There is still a trim shop at Browns Lane that makes up items like convertible hoods and the many minor items of interior trim required for all cars, such as arm-rests.

There is still a sawmill at Jaguar where all wood veneer is selected, cut, matched and heat treated onto special substrates for lightness.

All trim is brought to the line as needed for specific car orders but is fitted again by hydraulic assist arms to ease the burden of weight.

Quality is vital to Jaguar and there is a Management Control Centre in the assembly hall where all the key indicators on quality, volumes produced, safety issues and so on are logged and discussed and appropriate action is taken.

Most of the manual effort is now taken out of car assembly. Even the alloy wheels and tyres are hydraulically assisted onto the hubs and the wheel nuts are tightened to an exact torque figure.

The final mating of transmissions with bodyshell is also automatic, with the body lined up on lasers and no risk of damage.

The final line where cars are thoroughly checked before despatch.

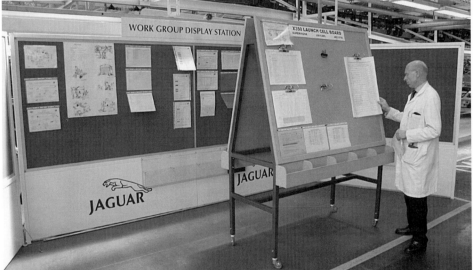

Work progress stations on the line where indicators are kept of group progress, and faults are identified and rectified so that everyone can be responsible for the ultimate quality of every car produced.

The road test area where cars go through various checks and drivers take the cars out on a local route as a final confirmation that they are ready for their new owners.

The ultra-modern service department still within the Browns Lane complex.

The cafe-bar area near reception where visitors to the factory can relax.

The gallery has a variety of exhibits and interactive displays for visitors to browse before taking a factory tour.

Jaguar and the Surrounding Area

All roads still lead to Jaguar and the city has numerous signs indicating the route to the Browns Lane plant. Compare the following three modern views with their parallel pictures on the endpapers.

This is the junction with Holyhead Road and Birmingham Road with the lane to Allesley village on the left and the specially built Coundon Wedge Drive in the centre.

This is Lockhurst Lane, leading directly to the old Foleshill factory. Little has changed, even the bus stop still exists, compared to the earlier picture.

183

Another modern view to compare. This is Radford Road facing towards the centre of Coventry with Heathcote Street on the left. The actual building which displayed the old Jaguar sign has long gone.

The factory photographed from Browns Lane showing the new office complex.

The original office complex still in use today at the rear of the recently completed frontage. A works canteen is sited here and if you look carefully you can still see camouflage on the walls from World War Two.

The vast assembly hall at Browns Lane, little changed from the 1950s and where most of the fire damage occurred in 1957. At the far right is what is called 'Craigs Folly' – a lean-to area that was erected when Peter Craig was plant director to ease the burden of deliveries in bad weather.

The full length of the assembly hall can be seen in this picture taken from the other end of the road.

The University of Coventry renamed one of its buildings, the Q Block in Gosford Street, Jaguar House, in recognition of the work and involvement Jaguar has had with them in Coventry. It encloses the university's School of Engineering and is also used by Jaguar staff for study.

Bibliography

Balfour, Chris *Roads to Oblivion* Bay View (Motorbooks), 1996.

Clausager, Anders *Jaguar, A Living Legend* Brian Trodd, 1990.

Clayton, Ken *Jaguar, Rebirth of a Legend* Century, 1988.

Collins, Paul *British Car Factories from 1896* (in association with Michael Stratton), Veloce Publishing, 1993.

Edwardes, Michael *Back from the Brink* Collins, 1983.

Frostick, Michael *The Jaguar Tradition* Dalton Watson, 1973.

Hassan, Walter *Climax in Coventry* Mercian Manuals, 1975.

Long, Brian *Standard, the Illustrated History* Veloce Publsihing, 1993.
  Daimler & Lanchester, A Century of Motoring History Longford International, 1995.

Montagu, Lord *Jaguar* Quiller Press, 1961.
  Daimler Century Patrick Stephens, 1995.

Porter, Phillip *Sir William Lyons, the Official Biography* (with Paul Skilleter) Haynes Publishing, 2001.
  Jaguar, the Complete Illustrated History Haynes Publishing, 1984.
  Jaguar, Project XJ40 Haynes Publishing, 1987.
  Jaguar, History of a Classic Marque Sidgwick & Jackson, 1988.
  Jaguar E-type, the Definitive History Haynes, 1989.

Skilleter, Paul *Jaguar, the Sporting Heritage* Virgin, 2000.
  Jaguar Saloon Cars Haynes, 1980.
  Jaguar Sports Cars Haynes, 1975.

Smith, Brian *The Daimler Tradition* Transport Bookman, 1972.
  Vanden Plas Coachbuilders Dalton Watson, 1979.
  Daimler Days (2 Volumes) (JDHT), 1996.

SMMT *The Motor Industry of Britain Centenary Book* Society Of Motor Manufacturers & Traders, 1996.

Thorley, Nigel *Jaguar, the Complete Works* Bay View (Motorbooks), 1996.
  You & Your XJ-S Haynes, 2000.
  You & Your XJ40 Haynes, 2002.
  Great Cars – Jaguar E-type Haynes, 2001.

Sutton Photographic *History of Transport (Jaguar)* Sutton (Haynes), 1998.

Turner, Graham *The Car Makers* Penguin Books, 1963.
  The Leyland Papers Eyre & Spottiswoode, 1971.

Underwood, John *The Will to Win* W.H. Allen, 1989.

Whyte, Andrew *Jaguar, the Definitive History of a Great British Car* Patrick Stephens, 1994.
  Jaguar XK – Forty Years On Aston, 1988.
  Jaguar, Sports, Racing & Works Competition Cars To 1953 Haynes, 1982.
  Jaguar, Sport, Racing & Works Competition Cars From 1954 Haynes, 1987.

Wood, Jonathan *Wheels of Misfortune* Sidgwick & Jackson, 1988.

Index

Motor Industry Research Association 72
Motor Panels Limited 21
Motor Panels Ltd 38, 40, 44
Mulliner 95
Mundy, Harry 120
Museum of Road Transport 161
National Advisory Council 58
National Enterprise Board 125
National Exhibition Centre 149, 170
National Union of Vehicle Builders 66
New Series XJ6 124, 167
New Zealand 57
Newsome, Alan 116
Newtherm Oil Burners Limited 111
NSPCC 166, 168
NSPCC Kids In Coventry Appeal 168
Orr, Hamish 140
Oxford 48, 54, 155
P. J. Evans Limited 18
Paris Motor Show 82
Parkes, Mike 133
Pininfarina 130
Poppe Ltd 30, 20
Premier Automotive Group 170
Pressed Steel Company 16, 54, 59, 82
Prince Andrew 147
Prince Charles 139, 147
Prince Edward 58
Princess Diana 139, 147
Princess Margaret 168
Privilege Ford Purchase Scheme 162
PSV 94
Putman, Roger 167
Queen Mother 98, 147
Queens Award 150
RAC 65
Radford Engines 127
Radford Sports 99, 171
Ram, Karan 7
Randle, Jim 156
Rankin, Ernest 30, 52, 55
Reid, Beryl 98
Reitzle, Wolfgang 170
Rialto Casino 56
Riley 25, 72, 110-11, 116
Roadliner 104
Robinson, Geoffrey 123-4, 126, 133, 144
Rolls-Royce 28, 32, 79, 111, 136
Rootes Group 38, 60, 79, 153
Rossenthal, Lou 116
Rover 60, 62, 115-16, 119, 125, 127, 130-1, 170

Rover V8 131
Rowland, Sir Archibald 62
Rubery Owen 33-4, 44
Rutherford & Stanton Ltd 79
Ryder, Sir Don 125
Ryder Report 125-6, 130
Sankey 34, 155
Savage, Brian 146
Scheele, Nick 163-4, 166-8, 170
Scorpion 108
Scotland 60, 149
Shadow Factory Project 50, 60-2, 91-2
Shorts Stirling 48
Sigma 170
Silverstone 56, 137
Simpson, Julia 7
Smart, Pat 167
SMMT 58
Solihull 125, 127
South Africa 57, 95
Special Vehicle Operations Department 165
Spitfire 43, 48
SS Car Club 30
SS Cars Limited 15, 30, 32, 38, 45, 47, 111
SS Jaguar 15, 32-4, 39-40, 42-43, 45, 56, 58, 128, 135
SS Jaguar Drophead Coupé 39, 135
SS Magazine 30
SS Queen Elizabeth 50
SS1 15, 28-33, 39
SS1 Airline 39
SS1 Coupé 39
SS1 Coupé Sal 39
SS1 Drophead Coupé 39
SS100 135
SS1s 30, 34
SS2 15, 28-31, 39
SS2 Coupé 39
SS2 Tourer 39
SS2s 30, 34
SS80 28
SS90 Sports 39
Standard Motor Company Ltd 28, 79
Standard Nine 28-9
Standard Nine Swallow 39
Standard Sixteen 28
Standard Sixteen Swallow 39
Standard Swallow 23, 28
Standard Triumph 13, 116, 130
Standards 28, 41, 80, 94, 117, 151, 166, 170
Stirling 43, 48
Stockport 14